Go It Alone!

Go It Alone!

The streetwise secrets of self-employment

GEOFF BURCH

Thorsons
An Imprint of HarperCollins*Publishers*

Thorsons
An Imprint of HarperCollins*Publishers*
77–85 Fulham Palace Road
Hammersmith, London W6 8JB
1160 Battery Street,
San Francisco, California 94111–1213

Published by Thorsons 1997

1 3 5 7 9 10 8 6 4 2

© Geoff Burch 1997

Geoff Burch asserts the moral right to
be identified as the author of this work

A catalogue record for this book is available
from the British Library

ISBN 0 7225 3460 4

Printed and bound in Great Britain by
Creative Print and Design (Wales), Ebbw Vale

To my best friend and wife, Sallie, who by waking me at 3 a.m. every day to tell me the book needed finishing, helped to get the job done. Also to all the Go-it-Aloners that I know, who not only inspired me, but have become my friends as well.

Contents

Introduction

Despite the fact that I am supposed to be some kind of corporate guru, I have always enjoyed spending a little time helping out with small-business start-up schemes. What prompted me to write this book was the experience of addressing the 'I want to do my own thing' contingent of an outplacement scheme. The thinking behind such projects seems to be that, when all else fails and a 'proper' job can't be found, you have to go off and start a business of your own.

There was a time when, if you got caught fiddling your dole or social security money, you could avoid further action by signing off. There was then an opportunity to go on the Enterprise Allowance scheme, which at the outset was a few quid a week, no questions asked, while you got the enterprise on its feet. This meant that I was confronted by a room full of those of the buccaneering spirit, to put it mildly. We would talk of selling oneself, the minimum red-tape requirement to prevent embarrassing prosecutions, and how to avoid converting all income into alcoholic beverages. You may feel that this was a recipe for disaster, but in fact they all did rather well in their own way, and it was my future delegates that have caused the most concern.

In recent years, it is the middle classes that have taken the hammering as regards jobs. As the bloody slaughter of middle management goes on, I now walk into an entirely different atmosphere. Instead of the nose rings, the creak of black leather, the abusive T-shirts, and pungent aroma of ganja and engine oil,

I am now met by Prince of Wales check, shoes that shine like new conkers, a row of very sharp pencils, folded arms, and an atmosphere of hurt bewilderment. I ask each delegate in turn what brought them here, and what their plans are for the future.

I hope that this book is going to be a great adventure for you. Part of it will be based on the replies received from these poor unfortunates. We will examine what can be done to secure a rewarding future for them and us, but let's save the really juicy bits for later and just have a quick glance at what they say:

'You, Frank.'
'Well, I was made redundant from my position of Resources Director for International Trip Wire.'
'And your plans?'
'I plan to become a consultant.'
'George?'
'I plan to become a consultant.'
'Janet?'
'I plan to become a consultant.'
'Derek?'
'I plan to open a tea shop.'
'Don't tell me,' I say, pinching the bridge of my nose in the style of all stage psychics I have ever seen, 'You are going to call it the Mad Hatter's Tea Shop.'
A gasp of astonishment, 'How on earth did you know?'
'Oh, just a lucky guess, I suppose.'

Lambs to the slaughter, doomed every one of them. But do you have to be doomed? Is there any hope? It's tirade time!

Professor Charles Handy writes some great books, and in a recent 'good guru guide', he was named as the philosophical champion of the damaged middle classes, but he says society must change. Well I agree, but it won't. It's like someone striding around the deck of the *Titanic* shouting, 'Ban all icebergs'. These books are gentle, reassuring, and comforting, but empathy is not what is needed on that listing deck. Me, I would dress in feminine attire and shout 'Women and children first'. In other words, if the circumstances won't change, then we must, and I intend to show you how to survive and survive well by hook or by crook.

WHY BE SELF-EMPLOYED?

When doing my outplacement guruing, I often encourage people to consider self-employment. This idea is often met with an enthusiasm that is tempered and even quashed by the fear of the unknown and of the obvious insecurity. I continue to encourage because, while I am familiar with the worry of not knowing where the next job is coming from and the feeling of doom when I consider my overdraft, I also know that the benefits outweigh the disadvantages. To my pleasure, I saw one of my former delegates some 18 months on. She had pockets that bulged and overflowed with large-denomination banknotes, she drove a fabulous convertible Rolls Royce, and with her were two Chippendale-style companions who pandered to her every need.

'So, it's going alright then?' I asked her.
'Oh yes,' she grinned. She was a godsend – I could use her as the example for anyone to be self-employed. 'It's clear why you are self-employed,' I said, 'It's all that lovely money.'
'Nah,' she replied, tossing a few handfuls of tenners casually into the air. 'I'm not interested in money.'
'That wonderful car then?'
'No, not bothered.'
'Then it's obvious, it's the adoring manservants.'
'Nope, I can take them or leave them.'
'Then why on earth are you self-employed?' I asked.
'Job security,' she replied with a big cheesy grin.
      Now that had really got me stumped. I believed I knew every conceivable benefit of self-employment, but job security has not exactly been top of the list. She went on to explain that all her working life she had been a faithful manager for a fizzy drinks company, getting up at six in the

morning to be the first in, and being the last to go home. She told me that she would watch the lazy guy with whom she shared an office doing his lottery numbers, organizing the staff bowling team and generally wasting time.

'For every pound I earned through my sweat, half would subsidize this moron. It wasn't fair. I was so loyal and conscientious, I would wake in the night thinking of fizzy drinks. Then one fateful day, someone at head office said, "Let's shut Milton Keynes," and I had no job. Was that security?' she asked. 'Listen, now I'm self-employed, I'm hardly likely to wake up one morning and make myself redundant, am I? Do you know why they shut my plant? Because they had a one-third drop in business and I happened to be in the third that got the chop. Last year I made £300,000. If my business drops by a third I'll have to struggle by on £200,000 – poor me! If you're self-employed, you're never unemployed. Skint, maybe, but never unemployed, and that's what I call secure.'

This really shook me up. Why do we believe that doing our own thing is less secure than a 'proper' job. Do you really think that your lords and masters are better at finding profitable work than you are, that they could handle money more efficiently, produce better quality to more markets or impress more people? Perhaps it is the business skills and experience that make the difference.

The answer is simple. Just learn those few extra skills and trust yourself more than your bosses, past and present, and I assure you that self-employment is secure employment.

WHAT ARE YOU WORKING FOR?

Go-It-Aloners work for different things. It is Tuesday afternoon and you are at the cinema. Do you feel guilty for not working? You do? Then you are no Go-It-Aloner yet.

I spoke to a friend, who is working himself very successfully to an early grave, about what he was working to achieve. He pointed proudly to his new £40,000 Jag.

'Forget your £40 per hour call-out charge,' I said to him, 'After tax, you probably clear about £10 per hour. That car costs 4000 hours of your life. That is 100 working weeks or, if you like, two years. If I pinched £40,000, I wouldn't expect more than a two-year sentence, and you have cheerfully sentenced yourself. Wouldn't it be nice to have two years of free time?'

High-flyers die of stress. Say they earn £100 per hour – with a more modest lifestyle they could put in four hours on a Monday morning and have the rest of the week off.

THE VERY STRANGE ACCOUNT

A friend, who is a highly paid auditor, does this, only he does it by the year, not the hour. He works like fury for three months doing his auditing for £12,000 a month. He spends a gentle three months on crazy but cheap business ideas that, strangely enough, make a lot of money, probably because he doesn't care. Isn't that always the way? He then spends six months living like a beach bum in Barbados. He lives in a modest home, and drives an awful rat heap of a car. The side-effect of this leisure time is what seems like dozens of happy children for whom he has all the time in the world. He says that we are born with a very strange bank account full of the most valuable thing in the world. We can draw and draw on this account and use its contents for any purpose we wish, but when it is empty, it is empty and cannot be replenished. We never know what balance is remaining because there are no statements. This account we are born with is filled with time – something we should not swap too readily for cash. After all, death is in effect temporal bankruptcy, and no money in the world will bring time back.

My buddy with the Jag asked me what he would do with all that free time. What did you do with your long summer holidays as a kid? I built dens and cooked camp-fire teas. What are you doing at this moment? Whatever it is, wouldn't you rather be cooking a sausage on a stick, riding your horse across the hills – you are a long time dead.

The serious aspect of this for the Go-It-Aloner is that, to start with, the work may be patchy, and if there is a small mortgage, a cheap car (or no car at all), no overheads or big leases, you can survive very well on a small income. Then you don't need to worry, and you can enjoy the leisure time. Of course, you can have bumper harvests, but don't buy the Jag. Think camel, and fill your hump, then if the work dries up or becomes too boring to do for a while, you can survive very nicely for as long as you like.

THE VOICE FROM THE OTHER SIDE

Sometimes stress is calculated by giving score numbers to certain life events: moving house 3, redundancy 7, loss of a spouse 8, theft of a motorcycle 9, dying 10. As any of these events threaten, we become stressed, and you may have noticed that death scores quite highly. People try to alleviate this stressful fear of dying by trying to find out if there is life after death. Great comfort can be gained by allowing a medium to receive messages from the other side. We love to hear tales of near-death experiences with tunnels of light and meeting old friends and relatives.

When I meet those who have experienced 'career bereavement', whether they have jumped or were pushed, they are undergoing a life change that some compare to death, and their questions are the same. Is there life after the event?

I have lived as a business guerrilla for nearly all my working life, and not only is there an afterlife, but it is a great life of milk and honey. So, let me be the voice from the other side – your spirit guide.

STRAP ON YOUR BEANS AND FOLLOW ME

When we were all terrified by the prospect of a nuclear holocaust, someone said that when the end of the world comes, we need nothing but a rucksack full of beans, a bicycle and a pump-action shotgun. For the moment, the nuclear holocaust threat has receded a bit, and the Armageddon we are faced with is a commercial one. Maybe the fallout has struck you, or perhaps you have had enough time in the trenches. If that is the case, what is the commercial equivalent of the bike, the beans and the shotgun? Harry Harrison, the great science-fiction writer, created a character based, he said, on the rats that, throughout history, have survived well and even thrived in the wainscot of society. But now, he said, we have a stainless steel society, so we need to be 'Stainless Steel Rats'. Up against the superpowers from the USA to the USSR, the raggedy shadow with a powerful weapon on his back has taken them on and won. From the Vietcong to the Mucha Haden, the ultimate victor has been the guerrilla. This can work in business. Travel light, live off the land and strike from the shadows. You have a great future assured. Victory will be yours, if only you can learn to GO IT ALONE!

Look Before You Leap – The Philosophy Bit

I want to take you by the hand and lead you up the rocky but golden pathway to success, but it might be a good idea to clear the air a bit, and decide just what success is.

I hope that, whichever runway you choose to take off from, you will reach the cruising altitude of your choice and arrive at the destination that you want to, because that is the major benefit of self-employment. It sets you truly free. But to start with, freedom can be a difficult thing to deal with and is really quite frightening.

There is a very cruel training trick used on elephants which consists of taking a young elephant and chaining it securely to a stake. The creature is then beaten and shouted at in an attempt to drive it from the stake. No matter how hard the terrified animal tries, it cannot break the massive chain that holds it. In fact, it would hurt itself trying. After days of doing this, the animal learns to stop trying to escape its tormentors because the pain they can inflict is less than that of its shackles. From that day onwards, people are amazed to see the elephant trainer push a single wooden peg into the ground and loosely wind a light piece of chain around it, and the animal's foot. Everyone can see that, if it wanted to, the elephant could just walk off with virtually no impediment. What secures it is not the chain, but its own fearful memories.

Whatever has led you to decide to do your own thing – whether you were pushed or whether you jumped, if your chain was cut off or if you snapped it yourself – you are now free. This freedom is not only fun, a thing of the purest joy if handled correctly, but it is also the vital component that makes the self-employed succeed against their employed competition. It is what makes the GUERRILLA able to defeat the regimented troops every time. The problem is that the average squaddy, when separated from his platoon, is soon a victim of the jungle, and would not consider firing his weapon unless ordered to do so. One of the keys to this fellow's survival is a bit of jungle training and the belief that he is free to make decisions. After a lifetime of discipline and order, we can find ourselves – like the elephant and the lost trooper – cut loose and unable to cope.

I know of a large insurance company where pay and conditions are apparently excellent, but once in at 9 a.m., you are not allowed out until 5 p.m., not even to buy a newspaper or whatever. They have been 'downsizing' recently, and their employees are bereft. Some feel that they have lost the structure that held their life together. I suppose being whacked with the ringmaster's stick to stand on an upturned tub on your hindlegs, or standing to attention by your bed at 6 a.m., can eventually become reassuring, but it is not really my bag, and it shouldn't be yours. This freedom to act as you want is not just a pleasure but the vital ingredient to your success. It just doesn't feel like that at the moment. Perhaps you need a bit of jungle training and permission to shoot at whomever or whatever you wish, metaphorically speaking, of course.

I am not necessarily talking about the sort of 'I want to be free, man' hippy-type freedom, but a type of business freedom which allows you to be frighteningly efficient. Having said that, there is nothing wrong with the hippy bit either – perhaps it's time you had a bit of freedom 'man'. Perhaps it would be cool to leave the work until Sunday so you can crawl around on your hands and knees being a tiger at your kid's birthday party on Tuesday. We will do our Zen mind and spirit bit later, but I must say that one of my biggest hurdles is getting over the freed wage-slave guilt at having a bit of time to just enjoy living. Anyway, I digress, it is back to efficiency for a bit.

A case that amused me and illustrates the point perfectly concerns a monster-sized public utility that was down-sizing, rationalizing, restructuring, becoming a flat organization and, not to put too fine a point on it, laying people off. The euphemistically titled 'human resources' department, which rarely appeared to be either human or resourceful, decided that to salve the guilt pangs of the powers that be, it would be a ripping wheeze to hold an outplacement training programme. They managed to find a wispy, ethereal American woman who could talk on getting in touch with your anger and disappointment in a high-pitched squeaky way. I am sure it was most valuable but I feel that the obligatory diet of non-aggressive rice and pulses was pushing things a bit too far. They also found bluff types who talked about investing one's redundancy lump sum for a happy early retirement. This unfortunately seemed to involve wearing a blazer with a badge on it, finding bowls and caravanning fun, and being an expert on the discomfort of haemorrhoids. To the company's horror, there was a small group of wild anarchists who felt that it might be nice to be self-employed or start their own business.

You notice I separate business and self-employment. The reason for this is that they are different. Sure, there are self-employed business people, but you don't have to have a business to be self-employed. In fact, you are just about to get me on to one of my favourite hobbyhorses, because I can't get the outside world to appreciate this, particularly the banks who have this 'If you don't work for somebody, then you are a business' mindset which, as we will discover, causes all sorts of problems – some for the world at large and some inside our own heads. I am aiming this message at everybody, from those in total despair as in 'If no one else will employ me I suppose I shall have to employ myself', to the self-assured 'I can do a better job of employing my talents than anyone else'. I find that I tend to read books like this one in the bathroom or when I am about to nod off, so it's unlikely that you will gallop through page after page. So for now, have a think until the next time you pick up this book about the sort of employment you will be offering yourself. We will talk together on that subject later.

Back to the outplacement course. As I mentioned in the Introduction, I can cope with the Hell's Angels, the rogues, the footloose and the fancy free – they have all been living off the land and know the game. It's another thing to be faced with a room full of suits, sharpened pencils and bewildered expressions of badly bruised egos, or, to quote the words of an old pop song, 'the lost and the lonely'.

The first step for me is to find out what everyone is capable of and then what they want to do. The flash term in the land of management speak is a 'skills audit', so I won't use it. Most of the gathered group believe that, as they have degrees and training in high-energy nuclear physics, satellite navigation techniques or supersonic weapons ballistics, that it would be some kind of waste not to continue using these skills. I concur most strongly with these views and, as you will see, I am a great fan of a discipline called asset marketing. Sure, one of your marketable assets is your skills, training and experience, but if that happens to be high-energy physics, probably the only market is the industry that you are just leaving, which kind of narrows the field. The result is that this group of the lost and the lonely tend either to offer themselves as consultants to their ex-industries, or have sadly unrealistic plans for business idylls that will reunite them with their drifting spouses and grow roses round the door of their country tea shop.

There are cheerful exceptions, of course, and I remember going from glum face to glum face to even glummer face until I encountered a chubby middle-aged character with a grin from ear to ear.

'What are your skills?' I asked.
'I'm a doctor of thermodynamics,' he replied.
'Your plans?' I yawned.
'I'm opening a poodle parlour,' he grinned smugly.

He had completely wrong-footed me, and when I had regained my composure, I asked where that idea had come from. It turned out that his passion was poodles, and the artistic clipping of said poodles, but all his life he had been told he could do better. His mum had mistaken his superb academic ability for a desire for an academic life, and subsequently his wife continued to tell him how fortunate he was to have such a respected position. Of course, a successful thermodynamicist doesn't throw it all up and open a poodle parlour. He was trapped by his own intelligence and his family's need for the status his job brought. The redundancy was a godsend; it presented his wife with a *fait accompli*, and him with the opportunity he needed. I met him later and am glad to say his dream had come true. The poodle business was a success, he was happy and his sceptical family were delighted to discover the cheery contented man who had once been the cheerless wage slave.

By the way, you may have noticed I described the poodle business as a success. Are you reading this book to find success for yourself? Do you know what it is? When I ask people about success, they have a frightening habit of drivelling on about palm-fringed shores and stretch limousines. But some time ago, when I had been self-employed for just a few years, things in my eyes weren't so good. The bank statement used to arrive literally smouldering and accompanied by a distinct smell of sulphur. Every month was a battle to survive, and then I met a respected business colleague who introduced me to a companion as a successful business man. I got him on his own, and asked him where he had got the successful bit from.

'How long have you been in business, Geoff?' he asked me.
'About four years.'
'And you are still here. I call that successful.'

Maybe success could be as little as paying the bills, having a modest holiday once in a while and, most importantly of all, guaranteeing yourself employment for as long as you want it.

As we have already seen, people attending outplacement schemes generally follow the usual trend and try to offer their services as consultants. Sometimes a little too much downsizing takes place within a company, and a number of quite useful babies get discarded in the rationalized bath water. The company then finds it actually needs the expertise of some of the people it has let go. I ran an outplacement scheme for one company which experienced such a scenario. After the redundancies had been made, the managers walked into one of their four-acre open-plan offices, switched on the lights and found, to their horror, that as each neon tube flickered into life, it illuminated empty desk after empty desk. One of their vital industrial processes was going haywire and they had disposed of everyone who knew anything about it. At this point they approached one of my delegates to see if he wanted to launch his consulting business by doing some work for his old outfit. The deal they offered was half of his old work for half of his old salary as a fee. He asked me what he should do and I suggested that he should snatch their arm off – after all, a bird in the hand, and so on. He duly undertook half his old duties for which he billed the equivalent of half his old salary. This all may seem ideal, but there was a bit of a fly in the ointment, in fact, a whacking great monster bluebottle of a fly, and that was that he achieved all this in just one day a month. His now client went ballistic. They felt that somehow they had been had. Did this mean that their new consultant wasn't doing a thorough job, or worse, did it mean that for the last 25 years their faithful employee could have handled his job in a mere two days a month? Whichever it was, they were well miffed and took our hero to task over it. The fact of the matter was that he had not been a consultant before and had quite surprised himself when the job had got done in such record time. He protested that he had worked hard all his working life, and that he had been just as diligent as he always was with his consultancy project. There are a number of strong lessons to be learned from this tale, some for the previous employer, some for the embryonic consultant, and some for us.

THE EMPLOYER'S LESSON

For the employer of consultants it must be accepted that there is a quite astonishing increase in efficiency. It is like one of those barmy perpetual motion machines that seem to conjure energy out of thin air, because the protagonists in this miracle don't have to be any more efficient to increase efficiency. In fact, in a business book I enjoyed reading recently (Tom Peters' *Getting to WOW*, I believe), a company discovered that when unusual, non-standard components were required by customers, up to 2,000 man-hours could be required to get the parts made and dispatched, and although blood-curdling, customer-terrifyingly high prices were charged, they still made a resounding loss. They decided this service should be cut, but then they discovered certain clients depended on it. The solution was to hand the whole thing over as a going concern to two spare employees who were free to wander where they wanted and charge what they like. The clients spoke to them direct, they put the bits in a Jiffy bag with a handwritten bill, and posted them off. The 2,000 hours were reduced to two hours. This is not a misprint. From order to dispatch in just two hours; they charged less and they made a huge profit.

Our consultant had discovered the same phenomenon by chance. He told us that, previously, when he needed disks for his computer, it could take days of form-filling, and weeks of waiting to get hold of them. He would use his considerable cerebral talents in the black world of office politics to get the equipment he needed or, if it came to it, equipment he didn't need, as long as it made him top gun office wise. Now he wanders up the road to Mr Patel's computer store, buys a handful of disks and wanders back. The whole thing – relaxing and ambling about in the sunshine, chatting to Mr Patel about football – takes a gentle 20 minutes or so, beating the previous best score by about $39\frac{1}{2}$ hours.

Keith Waterhouse wrote a wonderful book, *Office Life*, about a company called British Albion that, mysteriously, was more than willing to employ the lost and lonely, and unwanted middle managers, and to give them demanding clerical employment. Not to spoil the story for you too much, suffice to say that it was discovered to be a Government plot to prevent dissent. The whole company had got past the critical mass required to start generating work for itself to the point where it in fact did nothing else. Although that was a fiction, in a lot of companies the internal functions consume most of the company's power and bring British

Albion horribly near to the truth. I don't entirely understand the dynamics of this but it is a sort of diminishing return thing.

On Your Bike: The Advantages of the Solo Cyclist

I suppose because an organization has people in it, the structures needed to support those people become more demanding than the people, and require people to maintain them. Then there is another bind: knowing who is doing what and how hard they are doing it. If you use a bike as an example, it is quite easy to tell if no effort is being put into the pedalling because the machine stops and the feckless rider falls on their ear. If you are on a tandem, however, it is not so simple to tell if the other pedaller is not giving their all; in fact the only way to tell is to stop pedalling yourself to see if you both topple over. This strategy is often adopted by both riders, thus promoting a lack of trust and accusations of lack of weight-pulling from both sides. An argument against partnership if ever I saw one, but then partnership is an issue all of its own. The tandem as a machine is also becoming less efficient because of the strength required to take two riders. If the machine is built to take more riders still, the efficiency drops even further to virtually fatal levels.

Imagine, if you will, a cycle built for 50 people. The strength and weight of the tubing between the wheels would demand huge amounts of effort just to achieve any movement. That is, of course, if everyone is pedalling. How do you know who is or who isn't, or even if some are dead on their saddles! If speed were required, the decision may be taken to recruit extra pedallers but then more weight and machinery is required to accommodate them. This weight will probably exceed the new pedallers' ability to pedal, so at best they might drive only their own weight, at worst, more pedallers will be needed to compensate for the extra weight. If you could apply this analogy to large companies, the consequences become even more frightening. Take the effort of steering the thing. A massive amount of physical strength and great anticipation is required by the steerer, or even steerers, or even board of steerers. In fact, so much effort is required for this steering business, the people concerned certainly don't feel that they should be expected to pedal as well. This causes great resentment among the pedalling masses as all they get to look at is their boss's bum while they do all the work. The situation worsens if an emergency occurs up front, such as a child running out or a massive pothole, because the people on the handlebars will have to decide rapidly to apply the brakes. Of course, there is no time to inform the rest of the team who will keep pedalling. When the row about braking and pedalling breaks out, it is put down to a lack of communication.

I spend my life addressing groups who feel that their bosses tell them nothing, and addressing bosses who feel that their team is slow to react and resistant to new ideas. The solution is often felt to lie in training, working on the principal that if you could make your pedaller lean, fit and hungry, and capable of doing the work of two, you could shed your less able workers and get some kind of forward motion. That is in some way correct, but it means you must have a very harsh recruitment policy and an uncompromising redundancy regime. This is something that modern democracy tends to resist – in fact, it is a system that only really worked well in the Roman slave galleys – and although most current manufacturers would cheerfully embrace the use of the shackle, whip and drum, there is some protection for the workforce from this. In any case, there is an even more severe threat waiting, and that is the spectre of the catastrophic mechanical failure. If the bike buckles, then everyone is out of a job. So, if you want to cycle about as quickly as possible, what is the best role model? I would say the Tour de France. A few hundred cyclists all going like the clappers in the same direction. Big breakdowns and huge crashes take out just a few per cent, but that big amorphous thing that is the peloton just thunders on. You couldn't put that lot on one huge machine. In other words, nothing can ever be more efficient than pedalling your own bike. It also takes care of the fitness issue. When you see some of the old fossils still pedalling about, however sedately, at their own pace, you have to accept that they will reach their destination. It is the same with us self-employed. Some are still in the race, some move along at an efficient pace, and others just do what they need to do to get themselves about. There is no need for early retirement – you just ease up a bit, and it doesn't cost the consumer of your work a penny more.

The Smaller the Better: The Danger of Arming the Peasants
The huge economic return that is created by the simple concept outlined above has not escaped the powers that be in the wonderful world of commerce. But as they try to embrace it, they are presented with a paradox: the more free a person is, the more productive they can be, but if you set everyone free, you don't have an organization any more, and your artisans have a frightening habit of selling their skills to the highest bidder. They think that an answer has been found in setting people free-ish, something like giving our poor elephant a longer piece of chain. The jolly jape that I refer to is the new business-speak idea of empowerment – an idea that has the lords and masters trembling in their boots. It is like being told the best defence is to arm the peasants but then wondering what would happen if they turned on you.

'Well, don't really load their guns.'
'But what if we really are attacked?'

That is the key question. I met one of these 'empowered' staff the other day, when I stayed in a modern motorway motel. You get a pleasant but plain modern room, with a shower and colour television, but the food is supplied from the fast-food outlets on the site and was, quite frankly, horrible. There is not a lot you can do, because all payment is in advance and it is tricky to raise Cain at the reception because there isn't one. Then imagine my excitement to discover that, in the interests of customer care, the company had installed a smartly uniformed hostess to wave us goodbye at kicking-out time. The customer-care implant had been installed in her memory circuit and we were treated to:

'I'm Suzy, your hostess. May I thank you for staying at Goulag Lodge and ask you if everything was alright?'
'No, it wasn't. Last night's meal was truly foul.'

The reaction was astonishing. There was nothing in the manual to suggest that the customer would reply in such a fashion to this oft-repeated mantra. She said 'Oh' and her head clicked involuntarily in a sort of android-does-not-compute way. The solution was easy. She looked past me and said to the next person in the queue:

'I'm Suzy, your hostess. May I ...'

She was the classic peasant with the unloaded gun and I had called her bluff. What should she have done? The solution that I see as the best is also the one that gets large corporations baying for my blood because I believe it should go like this:

'I am sorry you were disappointed. What would you like us to do for you Sir, to put things right?'
'Well, I don't want to pay for it for a start.'
'Of course not, Sir. Please allow me to return the cost of the meal, and I invite you as our guest to give our restaurant another chance.'

With that, she opens the till, gives me £25 in cash, and a coupon for a free meal. This is the sort of subversive stuff that throws the captains of industry into fits of hysteria and get us into the very muddy waters of complaints, complaint handling and the relationship with the customer. The theory is that if the customer sees you as a soft touch, they take advantage. Well I don't think so, and in the case of the self-employed, you need every customer you can get, and when you get them, you need to keep them. This little tirade has shown that the corporate dinosaurs are demonstrating a real weak spot on this empowerment thing. What an opportunity for you. As a free agent, no one could be more empowered than the self-employed, and yet the general public complain most about the bad service received from the self-employed. They often spend more, to do business with large companies for the sake of 'better service'. It bothers me when I speak to prospective self-employed people who say that the major advantage of being small is that the prices can be lower. Why? Surely the major advantage is that the service is better, and I believe in some cases the prices should be higher because of your uniqueness. Imagine Beethoven saying 'OK, I don't have the range of the big music companies, but I can do you a nice cheap symphony'. Well that is an attractive proposition.

THE LESSON FOR THE CONSULTANT

All of these opportunities are what makes self-employment so lucrative and so efficient, but it must be understood that just having a personal skill, however good, is not enough. You may be the greatest carpenter, beautician, consultant or aardvark breeder, but it will count for little if you cannot master the black art of the surrounding magic. If an unhappy customer asks for their money back, what should you do? Where do you find these customers? How could you charge them many times more than before and still keep them delighted? This is what has to be mastered before the thing starts to work. Take for instance our original consultant, the man who could do a fortnight's work in one day. Where did he go wrong? He was very plainly skilled at what he did, like I am sure you are, dear reader, but perhaps like you he believed one of the greatest fallacies of business. The one that states that if you build a better mousetrap than anyone else, the world will beat a path to your door. Without a bit of sales, a touch of pizzazz, some showbiz, you are going to get stuck with a load of unsold mousetraps.

The mistake he made with the project was believing that his skill was enough and that simply completing the task was all that was needed. We need to put on a show. Take the example of a circus act. They have been doing what they do all their lives, and they could make it look easy, but that is not the point. You don't get the Great Alfonso, the world's most daring sword-balancer, walking out in silence to stand under a single 60-watt bulb, balance a sword on his head, remove it and then walk off again. The band would strike up 'Sabre Dance', and powerful searchlights would flash and scan the arena until they transfixed Alfonso, who would then proceed to slash up fluttering tissues to demonstrate the laser sharpness of his sword. The lights would dim except for a single searing blue-white spotlight transfixing the Great Alfonso. With a drumroll slowly climbing to a thunderous climax, he hoists this terrifying weapon onto his head, but at the climax the sword slips and plunges into the stage, a hair's breadth from our hero's feet. The crowd gasps in horror and excitement. When he does succeed, the audience breaks into a frenzy of applause. The point is, he puts on a show. Every night he drops the sword on the first attempt. It should never look easy. When I chat with people who are toying with the idea of starting a small business or becoming self-employed, they seem obsessed with their levels of skill and the saleable value of that skill. Statements like: 'I am a fine carpenter, and as a one-man band, I can charge less than everyone else'. Where is the showbiz in that? Can you have the skill without the show? Tommy Cooper and most talented doorstep salespeople have certainly shown that a good living can be made by having the show without the skill.

I fear that you sympathize with our carpenter. I have seen so many ventures fail when wonderfully skilled and experienced people believe that this is enough. My son tells what I am sure is an apocryphal story, but is none the less apposite, about the day he started his long rocky path towards becoming a lawyer. On his first day at college, the students sat in the great hall in hushed expectation of golden words from the senior professor. 'You are to become lawyers,' he boomed, 'And as such you have a solemn duty to uphold the tradition of the profession.' He paused for effect and the students fidgeted nervously, wondering if that which was to be demanded of them was to be too great. 'The first golden rule of your duty to our profession is, never let the client know how easy it is.'

Making it Look Too Easy: How the Pied Piper Cocked it Up

Our friend who started this little tirade did exactly that. He let the client see how easy it was. That is the problem. When you have a great talent, it is all too simple for your customer to undervalue your efforts when you make it look easy. Look at the poor old Pied Piper. He made it look easy and didn't get paid. Because he didn't get paid, he was forced to take punitive action against the client by stealing their children. So at the end of this project, the Piper was unpaid and the client had also lost a great deal. If the Piper had been a modern consultant, he would have kept his trap shut about his knowledge of rats, his bizarre musical ability, and how swiftly and easily his magical powers would work. As you are, I know, a kind, sweet-natured person, who is only considering the possibility of Go-it-Aloning, it probably won't do you any harm to consider some of the excesses that a number of major consultants use. I know you may not approve, but you will have to go a long way in the greed stakes before you even start to catch up with them.

I was called in to sort out a project that had matured into a spectacular cock-up. It was a tough one and I put in a very steep price with a view to putting the client off, or to get some good compensation for a poisonous assignment. Obviously, I hadn't been in the game long enough because the client joyfully grasped my hand and started forcing wads of cash into my pockets whilst virtually sobbing with gratitude. The major damage had been done by a large firm of international business consultants who, over a period of a year, had not only upset the client's entire workforce and cocked up the management structure, but had also charged literally hundreds of thousands of pounds. I asked why these people hadn't been kicked out in the first month. 'We couldn't do that because they didn't know what they were doing to start with.' I thought I was going crackers. 'They didn't know what they were doing to finish with, but surely that is the main reason for getting rid of them.' You must understand that this was some time ago and I was still a little innocent in those days. My mouth just gaped as the client explained to me that these slick characters had informed him that, as they knew nothing about his business, he would have to pay them initially for a learning-curve project! They were then working on a consultant day rate of around £1,000, and although this is considerable, it is not unreasonable to expect a good freelancer to earn the same. What was unreasonable was what they called a 'day' and what they called a 'consultant'. It seemed that everybody there was a consultant, from tea boy to executive, and at the end of a 40-hour week of five eight-hour periods, each and everybody was expected to attribute £5,000's worth of time to some unsuspecting (or actually, by this time, very suspecting) client. The game seemed to consist of the best brains fronting up the sales pitch with the Jermyn Street shirts, Chanel suits and smoked salmon sarnies; and when you had bought, signed in blood, and worst of all, parted with the money, you got the real klutz who would do the project. Adding insult to injury, you paid large sums of money to educate this halfwit in the secrets of the company. This would be laughingly known as phase one (a bit like the Sting, I suppose). At the end of the learning curve came research and feasibility. This gave the consultants a chance to employ some of their very expensive chums at the company's expense. Action plan, implementation and review were supposed to come after this, but let's stop here. I am sure you didn't buy this wonderful book on securing a glittering future for yourself just to hear a tirade on the duplicity of City consultants.

So what have we learned that could be of value to us? I suppose the first person who really needs educating is the client or customer. We all do it. We buy ourselves a shiny car and because we want to be fastidious about its maintenance, we take it to the main dealer where we are greeted, we hope, by a smiling and charming service manager. But do you consider who will actually be working on the car? I should imagine the apprentices and less able engineers are given the simpler or less lucrative jobs. If someone passes through the garage's training programme and rises up through the ranks as far as a mechanic can, the chances are they will leave and start their own small repair business. We would describe this as a back-street operation and be less inclined to take our car to them, despite the fact they are probably a cheaper and far more competent operator. If the best mechanics leave to set up on their own, it stands to reason that they are better than the ones left behind.

This situation requires very careful analysis because it is the key to how our enterprise will make us money. It is the classic situation that was referred to earlier. On one hand we have a person of consummate skill who believes that any fool could see the benefit of using this skill at a budget price; and on the other hand, we have the potential customer whose perception is of a down-market 'back-street operation'. Are you in that position? Do you have a very special skill or a great idea to sell? If we go back to our dubious consultants, they managed to virtually reverse the situation by making a virtue of having no skill whatsoever. In fact, when I managed to interview one of these consultants, I asked him about this learning-curve thing. I told him that it wasn't too hard to believe the extent of their ignorance, but surely they must occasionally have some experience in the relevant areas. He gave me a huge wink and tapped the side of his nose with his finger. 'My dear boy, of course we have oodles of experience, but we don't want to let the client know that, now do we?'

I know all of this is excessive, but we should learn something from it. In the case of the Pied Piper for instance, try to imagine yourself in his position. As a long-term employee of Consolidated Pipering, Enchanting and Associated Sorcery Inc. PLC, you have been downsized out and decide to Go it Alone. A mate tips you off that Hamelin have got a bit of a rat problem. You know you can do rats standing on your head, so you toddle off to earn a few quid on what should be a fairly straightforward project. Of course, we all know what happened, but things could have been so different. You know how easy it is to get rid of the rats but the client doesn't have to. You arrange a meeting with the town council to agree a programme which would include a survey, report and possible feasibility study that would all generate fees. A clear pricing structure would be agreed, and you set out a schedule of payment that gives you most of the money up front. May I even suggest that the switched-on Piper might leave just enough rats to maintain a lucrative ongoing relationship? After all, you don't necessarily want to work yourself out of a job.

You should now be getting a whiff of the fact that there is more to this lark than just the core skills. In fact, in the next chapter we will see that you might not even need the core skills to succeed. We have to take our kernel skill and surround it with the succulent fruit that is the show, the sale, the surrounding magic. A great deal of this book will be dedicated to how you can create that magic, but as an itinerant 'help you to make your fortune' guru, the biggest hurdle I can find is the mental wall built of the solidest rock, which resists the idea of sales, marketing or anything that could be construed as froth and bubble. You will have to learn to sell to survive. The way your customers see you is what determines your profitability. Do you make something? Is it a wonderful, beautifully made thing? Then think about this quote from the salesmen's guru, John Fenton: 'Production minus sales equals scrap'.

Every Home Should Have One – If Only They Knew!

At one of my seminars, I was shown a beautiful carved wooden household thingy, a thingy that we would all be proud to own. The designer of this object didn't want to discuss sales, marketing or distribution. He declared that this novel and attractive idea would be the principal addition to anyone's home, and everyone would want one – a contention that was fully supported by the rest of the delegates who all said they would love one. Despite my pleas for caution, he blithely mortgaged his house to make thousands of these things. He wandered round a few shops who took a few of these things on sale or return, and he sat back to watch the cash roll in. The result was total and complete financial ruin, and those things were literally sold for scrap. Did I gleefully dance on his grave? Not at all. I was one of the few people to buy one, and once I got it out of its dreary grey cardboard box with cheap, amateurish illustrations, it has given me endless pleasure and delight. That is a sad tale, but the writing is on the wall for anyone who ignores its message.

Cut-price Brain Surgery: A Great Idea

Let's forget for a moment why you are starting this enterprise, and examine how you are going to make your mark against the competition. When you decide to make a purchase or to employ a contractor, how do you make your decision? On price, on quality, on availability? Why are people going to choose to do business with you? You have to have a competitive advantage, and despite the flack he has received, no one has been more correct in analysing the situation than Tom Peters in his book *In Search of Excellence*. I know that he and Robert Waterman aimed the book fairly and squarely at corporate America, but their bit on competitive advantage is even more appropriate for the business Go-It-Aloners.

OK, you are ready to start your enterprise; what will give you the edge? Price? I get a never-ending stream of people who insist that they will succeed because they can be cheaper due to lower overheads. This is a disastrous way of thinking. Cheap is unattractive to your customers. Who is going to employ a 'cheap' surgeon? Even if you move to the very bottom and start trading factory reject goods on weekend markets, I will lay odds that someone will come and undercut you.

The next option I get battered around the head with is the concept of the new idea – the one that no one else has thought of. Firstly, there are very few ideas that no one has thought of, and the fact that they are not about now is because they sank without trace. Let's assume for a moment that you really have made a breakthrough discovery – the big one, the one that will set the world on fire. A local chap discovered a wonderful toy. He made it in his shed and, despite his tatty packaging and lack of sales skills, this thing was so marvellous, people bought as many as he could make. It was pointed out to him that the large multinational companies were starting to move in like crocodiles slithering down the bank in the best of the old Tarzan movies. He was sure he was safe as the idea was patented, but he had underrated the tenacity of his competitor. To develop a new toy must cost many thousands or even millions, so why not gamble just a few thousand on a good patents lawyer to see if he can't knock holes in the other guy's patent. This they duly did and then flattened our poor toymaker with slick marketing, sharp advertising and worldwide distribution. Twenty years on, the toy is now one of the most popular in the world and is made by hundreds of firms. Meanwhile, our small toymaker wanders around still wondering what hit him.

Someone once said that pioneers are people who are found face-down in the dust with arrows in their backs. Don't think that I'm saying that new ideas don't work; it's just that they need no less effort than an established one, and although it is nice to be responsible for something new, don't ever depend on it to give you a competitive advantage.

Tom Peters set down the possible options and, like us, dismissed price and innovation, but then came up with a third which is the answer that we have all been looking for. He set it down like this:

Opportunities for Competitive Advantage:

1 Price
2 Innovation
3 THE WAY WE DO IT

That's right, THE WAY WE DO IT. It looks so simple, but just think about your favourite high-street store. Why do you shop there? Price? Can't be, there must be somewhere cheaper. Innovation? I bet they're not at the cutting edge. People then tend to start chuntering on about quality, but the store probably isn't at the cutting edge for quality, either. The reply is 'Well they are, for the prices they charge'. That is the answer. They balance professionalism, position, service, quality, presentation and price in a way that could only be described as the way they do it.

The only disagreement I have with *In Pursuit of Excellence* is that it seemed to be aimed at the corporate sector which will probably never learn, and yet I truly believe the lessons are much more appropriate to the business guerrilla. Much of the rest of this book is dedicated to helping us improve and benefit from 'The way we do it', and as I am assuming that funds are limited, your future fortune will lie with personal recommendation of your service, whilst you make a walloping great profit. A difficult but rewarding balance to achieve, so before we plunge on, let's just see what benefits this chapter has brought us.

POINTS TO PONDER

1 Think about the sort of employment that will make you happy – you may be doing it for ever!
2 If your new job is based on your old skills, your old employer may be your only new customer.
3 Pedal your own bike and go where you want, or stop pedalling and fall on your ear. It's your choice.
4 'Say, why don't we put on a show!' Don't forget that successful selling requires some pizzazz.
5 Never let the client see how easy it is.
6 Cheap isn't cheerful.

2

On Your Own: Now What?

I suppose the first questions have to be: why are you going out on your own, how much money do you want, and do you care what you do? There is a new thing that everybody in the States is raving about, called 'downshifting'. Basically, it means trading in a high-powered, high-earning lifestyle for a 'simpler', down-scaled life. It is a very West-coasty sort of thing and the core message is concealed in a lot of new-age mumbo jumbo. It seems to suggest that it is *de rigueur* to wear itchy handwoven underwear whilst eating tofu and walking everywhere on sandals made of recycled car tyres. Although the associated literature of this movement sometimes verges towards hysterical proselytizing, beneath it all are some strong and valuable messages for all us Go-It-Aloners, especially in this chapter where we decide what we are going to do to earn our crust. This all now gets a bit confusing and philosophical but there is a point, I promise you, so pin back your ears and bear with me. Firstly, we have to deal with this work to live/live to work thing.

ABOUT DOWNSHIFTING

Although I am making fun of downshifting, it is based on quite sound principles, and a little basic explanation here wouldn't go amiss. The ideas behind the American movement are not that new, and anyone in Britain who watched the television comedy series 'The Good Life' will have experienced the English version, which I suppose like all things British, has an element of class division in it. The Goods are a very well-educated, big-earning, luxury suburban couple who find that they can live on a peasants' income and still maintain middle-class values and, to some extent, lifestyle. The punchline and *raison d'être* is that this makes them happy.

The American version of downshifting, unsurprisingly, reflects a very American view which is intellectual Ivy League, hippy-driven, life-statement stuff, but in itself is far more practical and less dreamy than 'The Good Life'. In pure financial terms, it includes some very clever notions about auditing your life. For instance, how much time do you spend working? You may think you work eight hours a day, but how long does it take to travel to and from the office. You should also take into account the amount of time it takes you to get ready in the morning, and the wind-down period you need when you arrive home at night. So the eight-hour day is probably more like 12 or 14 hours, depending on the length of your journey. How much do you have to spend to go to work? Maybe an hour's wages from each day is spent on sending your suits to the dry-cleaners to look good for your job; maybe you work for two hours every day just to buy and run that smart car. Would you need such a smart home if it wasn't for the job? You may have to work for 60 hours a week just to pay the mortgage. You may think you earn £10 per hour, but when you take the above expenses into consideration, you really earn £4, and you are killing yourself.

The solution, America's 'simple living' pundits say, is to downshift, to reduce your personal consumption to a point where you work very much less, or even do no paid work at all, or do a job which is low paid but worthwhile. I touch on this a bit more in this chapter, but it is most important for you to understand that this is definitely not a book on downshifting, and I personally don't think too much of it, if only because the downshifting process itself seems to turn into a full-time job, which defeats the object. *Go It Alone!* is a survival guide, not a lifestyle guide, although I suppose from my point of view, self-employment does generate some kind of special lifestyle. Where downshifting is a great help is that its strategies can show us how to survive on nothing which, for that first year or so, you will be doing. So here endeth my lesson on downshifting. Now read on to see how it could help you survive.

WHY DO YOU WORK?

I am sure in your working life you will have gone beyond earning the price of a few bowls of simple gruel to put before your family as they sit in a rude homemade shelter, their eyes streaming from the smoking log fire. (Mind you, the downshifters would see that as a great lifestyle statement.) It is likely that you have small luxuries such as a television, alcohol, meals out or even holidays, but do you work because you want and need these things, or because they compensate you for the dismalness of work. Conversely, of course, a number of people so enjoy these things that they elect to do the most dismal jobs purely for the rewards. But what if the extras are just compensations? If you don't work, you don't need the compensations, and if you don't need the compensations, you may not need to work.

It is not out of the question, however, to love what you are doing, have stacks of free time, and generate buckets of money. Therefore, this could easily be the goal. If you simply enjoy the work and the free time but feel uneasy about the unaccustomed wealth, you could always send the surplus to me. One area our Californian chums have been very clever with is a 'lifestyle score'. This has certainly made me think, and having thunk, has made me even more of an evangelist for going it alone. I would like you to think hard about this, because although it is a tricky thing to grasp, it is the essence of everything we have been considering.

GET A LIFE – BUT WHICH ONE?

What they say is that people who have normal day jobs have two completely separate lives, with a very sharp cut-off between the two. You have a life with loves, laughs and interest, and after breakfast you put it on hold until the evening, while you spend the day as a bus driver, accountant or dress designer. Your family gets used to having a life with you, and one without you. You could be in deep trouble when you find out which one they enjoy most. Like retirement, self-employment can test families to the limit when one or other partner finds how tough it is spending 24 hours a day with their beloved. If you are still considering the rose-tinted temptation of that country tea shop, as you and your partner cheerfully share the labours of the day – chuckling, gambolling around like happy children in a sun-kissed meadow among the colourful butterflies – consider the time period required before you want to cut each other's throats.

I am torn here because I do believe that 'going to work' is an alien concept and historically a fairly recent thing. The downshifters try to compare the cost of things or the value of money to the life energy expended, which is OK as far as it goes. It was quite useful to us in the luxury car story where we could that the actual cost of the vehicle was two years of life energy. If, however, you go back in time, things alter somewhat. Take for example the village miller or blacksmith. The miller would probably run the mill non-stop just after the harvest, and when things quietened down, he and his son would clamber all over the mill doing a spot of maintenance. His wife's cheery face would pop out of a hatch somewhere on the body of the mill and call them in for their lunch, and they would sit around the table munching away at fresh-baked crusty bread and farmhouse cheese, and drinking strong ale. Perhaps on the table would be some great cogwheel from the mechanism, and over their leisurely meal, it would be decided that the smith should take a look at it. This would involve a cheery stroll to the village where the smith would appear in his workshop from a doorway that literally opened out of his kitchen where he had been enjoying a similar lunch with his family.

Now, if you could interview these people, they would maintain that they were always at work, but then at the same time, they were always at home. There weren't time and motion people after them, and there were no managers. They set a pace which suited them, perhaps lengthening their day but lowering their stress. In fact, the cogwheel incident is echoed in our electronic consultant's stroll to the computer shop. The problem is that your life partner did not marry a miller or a blacksmith, and the changes brought about don't just upset you, they can upset everybody. Upset is the main thing to avoid as the whole point of this is to have a measured life that generates anything you want or need without a great amount of stress and with a reasonable degree of entertainment.

It is unlikely that the miller would describe himself as a business man or an entrepreneur. He would just call himself a miller. If he were whisked off to the 20th century, he would have all sorts of problems as various organizations would try to categorize him into an employment group. As you start your enterprise, you will find that the banks sum up this ambivalent attitude perfectly, and unless we watch out, we can be sucked into their description and be misguided into taking the wrong route. The banks, you see, believe there are quite simply two sorts of customers: personal or business. From what I can see, business bank accounts for various reasons are more expensive and unwieldy than personal accounts, but as soon as you mention that you wish to be self-employed, the bank will describe you as a business, and insist that you have the appropriate account. It is not really the cost I object to, but the attitude, an attitude I may add that is shared by government departments. As soon as you cease being employed formally by someone else, you literally change species.

Although I wish to save the technical details for the appropriate chapter and I will accept that banks often offer better interest rates for business loans than they do for personal loans, I do just want to say that by carefully avoiding using my business account, I save around £1,000 a year in charges. In fact, some people even use private or building society accounts, but while researching this, I spoke to a bank and they told me that if they caught a customer doing that, they would insist that they opened a business account.

The point of all this is that when we are deciding what enterprise to embark on, we must acknowledge a difference between starting a business and employing ourselves. If banks stopped to think for a moment they would realize that there is great potential for them to make money from the third group, who should be described as people who employ themselves. These are often people who have left the shelter of formal employment where the employer organized the financial fringe – such things as holiday pay, pensions, health insurance and company cars. There are huge opportunities for banks to fill this role at great profit to themselves and great peace of mind for ourselves, but they don't seem to be able to get their heads round that, and keep wanting us to take expansion loans and file cash-flow forecasts.

On the subject of cash-flow forecasts, many years ago when I had a proper day job, I prepared a cash-flow forecast for our company to secure a loan for some machinery. The bank examined the columns of figures and declared the figure for predicted turnover too small to justify the borrowing so I crossed it out and rewrote one that was twice as big. There was a shocked gasp. 'You can't do that – where did you get that figure from?' I replied that I had got it from the same place as I got the other one. 'Out of the air. Everyone gets them out of the air unless they are clairvoyant.' 'I suppose they do, but you aren't supposed to let us see you do it,' sulked the bank.

This takes us into the serious area of the trouble you can find yourself in trying to finance your business schemes. Banks make their profit by lending money, and it is unlikely that they will lend to you unsecured. In other words, they will not lose, whatever happens to your enterprise. Therefore it is quite scary to consider that, even with the banks' liberal attitude, there are some business schemes that are so flawed that even they wouldn't lend for it, and yet the embryonic business person thinks the bank is stupid not to see the opportunities, and they finance from other, often more aggressive sources. Pull a stunt like that, and the chances are that you are doomed. If 'doomed' isn't an option that appeals, how can you avoid it?

REGINALD'S RENT-A-RODENT SYNDROME

Perhaps you could run your scheme past a few people and see what they think. The fly in this ointment is that you may not want to hear the truth, but then that doesn't matter because no one will tell it to you anyway. In my private life I am a born coward, and as a business consultant I am paid to lie, so if you asked me privately what I thought of your scheme, I would not have the bottle to say it stinks, but if you paid my considerable fee I would tell you that you are a genius and, for a further consideration, I would write a weighty report to prove it. None of this is much use because you need to know the truth, believe it and act on it, however harsh and unpalatable it is. We are not messing about here; we are talking about the rest of your life, and a bit of hurt pride mustn't stop us making the right decision.

If you think I am laying this on a bit thick then let me whisk you across the astral plane where in spirit, if not in body, you can join in on one of our 'start your own thing' groups. In the coffee lounge before the start, you have all had a good old chat between mouthfuls of sugary jam doughnuts and slurps of hot frothy cappuccino. As in any situation where a group are thrown together in a common situation, you will become chums. As you file into the seminar room, you will gaze in suspicion at the festering old hippy who is supposed to be counselling you on your future. When the group is settled, I leap up and ask each one of you your plan for the future. Each answers the predictable answers until we get to Reginald. There is always a Reginald.

'What's your idea, Reginald?'
'I do not wish to discuss it. It is a business coup that is so unique it will take the world by storm.'

I point out to him that this is why he is on the course, and unless he shares just a little of the secret we will not be able to help him guarantee its success. He eyes me with deep suspicion and then starts:

'I have a unique proposition for which I believe there is an unfulfilled niche which I could fill most profitably. I have decided to call my enterprise "Rent a Rodent".'

When I catch your eye you raise an eyebrow, and flicker a little smile. The little smile that says 'This man is an idiot'.

'Rent a Rodent, hey? What gave you the idea, and what makes you think it will work?'
'Well,' Reginald is picking up speed. 'From tragedy came opportunity. I went with the good lady wife for a short holiday, and on my return was shocked to discover that my entire collection of rare guinea pigs had passed over, and had in fact travelled to that great hutch in the sky. The cause was the neglect of my neighbour who had assured me of his support but on the day had let me down. I was devastated but a germ of an idea started to form. Instead of all the worry of ownership, people could rent our little furry friends. I would supply any type of rodent on a long or short term basis.'

How do I tell this man?

'What makes you think this is going to work? Have you done any research or attitude surveys?'

With the fanatical glint in his eye of a suicide bomber, he replies:

'I'm no fool you know. Virtually everybody I have spoken to has given a positive response, even my fellow delegates today have given a universal and enthusiastic thumbs-up, haven't you?' he says, fixing you with his gimlet stare.

Come on, be honest, what do you say? Are you going to be the one to tell him that he is barking mad. 'Great idea Reg,' you mutter. The result is that in six weeks time a knock will come at your door and there will be Reginald carrying a box, out of which through a slot in the front gazes a pair of malevolent red eyes, a long leathery tail hangs out of the back, and the whole thing emits a piercing 'eeeeek' noise. Reginald smiles the contented smile of the maniac on the loose and thrusts the box at you. 'You expressed a keen interest in one of our furry chums the last time we met.' As you leap back screaming, ask yourself why no one put Reginald straight much earlier on, and even more chilling, would anyone put you straight?

DO YOU REALLY WANT TO HEAR THE TRUTH?

This book was commissioned by my hyper-cheery mid-Atlantic editor to be an exercise in happy, positive thought about creating your ideal future, so I am just a tad reluctant to be depressing in case she doesn't pay me, but what the hell. The fact is, get it right and it can be the road to fulfilling every dream you ever had; get it wrong, and the word 'tragic' will take on a new meaning for you.

People frighten me. They literally mortgage their homes and everything they ever worked for to finance completely barmy schemes. Of course, your scheme isn't barmy, or is it? Would you really listen to me if I thought it was, and told you the truth? Joking aside, I promise that I do try. Reginald is an obvious caricature, but other disasters can be less obvious.

One delegate told me that he wanted to open a luxury handmade chocolate store. I said that other people had made a success of these but didn't he think that the market was getting a bit saturated these days. He told me that he had a cunning scheme. What he had in fact done was map the position of every chocolate store in the country in relation to population distribution. From this he had discovered a highly populated area that had no luxury chocolate shop. This happened to be the Rhondda Valley in South Wales, at the time one of the most economically depressed areas. When, I pointed out that the residents of the Rhondda might not have all that much spare cash for luxury chocolate and that the lack of competition from other chocolate stores was probably no oversight, this observation caused a surprisingly acrimonious reaction. This guy had borrowed against everything he had – his redundancy money, his home, his all – and yet the project was being lavishly equipped with not just the obvious choccy related items, but also with electronic do-das such as computers, sophisticated tills, copiers and faxes. I got so annoyed, we literally stood and bellowed at each other until he stormed out calling me a 'pillock'. Pillock or not, what was I trying to tell him? What am I trying to tell you? What was I to gain by raining on his parade?

The whole point of writing this book was to try and ensure your success. From a purely selfish point of view, I would like you to enjoy this book, use its advice to achieve the success you want, and then tell the whole world that the book is the secret of your triumph and that they should read it. I want to be pleased to meet you and not worried in case you've had a cock-up. I have a vested interest in you; your success is my success, so if this section contains some unpalatable news, it is best to face it now rather than face the bailiffs in a few years time. After all, you don't shout at a road map if it impassively indicates what a long and arduous journey you have ahead of you. At least it is a map, and if it is accurate and you don't try too much clever stuff, it guarantees that you will arrive at your destination. Imagine the consequence of someone publishing an optimistic map that left out the hills, dead ends and cliff edges, and then shortened all the mileages to give you a bit of encouragement. Your competitor with the real map would set out with a lot less enthusiasm than you, but it wouldn't be long before you got lost, worried and literally in fear of your life. Therefore, let's set out to a realistic destination with no illusions about how easy it is to get there.

DEVELOP THE COMMITMENT OF A FREEDOM FIGHTER

This book is supposed to compare the survival techniques and battle-winning methods of the classic jungle guerrilla to a person making their way in the jungle of commerce. The first area in which we have a potential for disaster is that the classic guerrilla is always some kind of fanatic who has a cause in mind, a focused goal. As they plunge from a palm tree with a necklace of live grenades, they cry out, 'Democracy for the peasants of Ruritania', or something similar. OK, come on, what will you cry as you plunge from your palm tree? 'I suppose anything is better than being on social security'? Doesn't have the same ring or feeling of commitment somehow.

It is vital to know why you are planning to Go It Alone. The first, and in these difficult times, most pressing reason is the need for paid employment to keep body and soul together. I think this is often one of the best and most successful reasons. The failure rate for new businesses is depressingly high, and often a great number of self-employed people drift back to 'proper jobs' despite having kept their heads above water. In a part of the gritty heartland of the USA, where doom statistically awaits the entrepreneur, small businesses do surprisingly well and are really becoming the engine room of the economy. Someone asked Tom Peters the reason for this phenomenon: why do the small businesses succeed? His answer was succinct: "Cause they gotta'. There will be no better reason for you to succeed than "Cause you gotta'. OK, let's examine 'gotta'. 'Gotta' what? Earn a living? Keep the wolf from the door?

THE SELF-EMPLOYED ARE A DIFFERENT SPECIES

I read the bible of the American downshifting movement, *Your Money or Your Life*, with some horror, not because of the radical things it was suggesting, but because of the surprise it expressed at what it had 'discovered'. The book wasn't wrong – I was. I hadn't realized the extraordinarily difficult rite of passage from the employed world to the self-employed world. It's all about the power you have to determine your own destiny. It may be hard for you to see as free spirits the scruffy bloke on the old moped who does people's gardens, or the girl with the beat-up van who goes around doing the pensioners' hair. Even more confusingly, they would not describe themselves as such, either. The situation is that they have literally evolved into another species with a totally different value structure, and we are going to have to get a bit philosophical to translate what is their definition of success.

If you have a well-paid job, you can have a nice lot of big debts and own flash things that may compensate you for the drudgery of your job. In fact, the purchase of compensations may be the only free choice that you can make. I know a lot of self-employed people who have luxuries that way exceed the dreams of the employed, but somehow it is different. If we translate the goods into life energy expended, we come to understand their real value. If I want a new car, I have to spend my money, which is inextricably linked to the expenditure of my life energy, as the Americans call it, or my time if you want to be a bit more prosaic. I can replace money, but not time, so maybe I will take the time and stuff the car. To my surprise, the other day I realized that I could upgrade my car and went off in a red mist to enjoy the almost sensual pleasure of buying the car of my choice. I came back a broken man. I had been away from it all for too long. None of the tin and plastic boxes turned me on; none were worth around a year of life energy. I came home in my old clunker, determined to keep it till it drops to bits and then to buy another heap to get about in.

So, be careful when you get into this life; be prepared to be changed, preferably for the better. Of course, the pendulum can swing the other way and great indulgence can be undertaken by the guerrilla in their leisure moments.

SAVE MONEY: BUY YOUR OWN AIRLINER

I have a friend who is a self-employed freelance engineer, but his proclivity is for aircraft. It must be understood that aircraft, even cheap aircraft, are very expensive, especially when you have a modest income, like my friend. And spending all your time fiddling with aeroplanes doesn't help your business because your client can never find you.

My friend had the opportunity to purchase a fairly large vintage aircraft, and although it cost many thousands of pounds, it was, in relative terms, a bargain. His wife, with whom he had a more than stormy relationship, railed at the whole idea and presented him with an ultimatum: 'Either that plane goes, or I do.' When I visited him in his modest modern home a few days later, I was surprised to see that the large picture window and wood cladding had been removed from the house and a propeller was protruding. I climbed over the rubble to find our chum sitting on a chintz sofa, up to his ears in oily machinery whilst simultaneously watching the television and eating cheese sandwiches and drinking beer from a tin. 'Where's the wife?' I asked. 'Gone,' he replied, grinning from oily ear to oily ear.

PEDALO POWER

Although my friend's tale has a relatively 'happy' ending, if you do value your partner be sure that they really do want to share this roller coaster adventure with you, and that they have had input into what they want out of it. Thus we move full circle and return to asking what you want from this. A lot of the available pay-offs are feelings such as contentment, excitement, freedom from worry, happiness, a sense of achievement and status. If there are a particular set of feelings that you crave, the employment you choose can be a simple means to an end.

Take as an example a person who, in my youth, used to make me sick with jealousy. He was tall, he was handsome, he was brilliant at sport and everybody loved him. His glittering career peaked with his success at becoming a professional footballer. But everything must come to an end, and with the vicarious joy of *schadenfreude*, we saw him retired early from football with an injured knee. Well, it must be supposed that where a meteoric rise ends, a slippery slope begins, and I always expected to find the ex-footballer lying in a ditch somewhere as a hopeless alcoholic. Imagine my surprise, then, and perhaps a little disappointment, when I saw a sun-bronzed apparition bounding towards me with a gorgeous beauty hanging adoringly on his arm. He was fit, happy and looked about ten years younger than me. Greeting me like a long-lost friend, he told me of his life after football.

'What have you been doing?' I asked.

'Pedalos, mate,' he laughed, slapping my back with the impact of a road accident.

He explained that with his pay-off from the football club, he had bought a fleet of pedalos on a beach in Majorca. I can't remember the exact figures, but it was something like 20 pedalos earning £50 an hour, 10 hours a day, 7 days a week, 7 months of the year, and that is at today's price.

'What is the drawback?' I asked, hopefully.

'Well, there is a nasty occupational hazard,' he replied. 'Yes, you get a sunburnt palm when you push it from under the beach umbrella for the money.'

'Aren't they a tie? What if you want time off?' There had to be a drawback.

'No problem. A kid from the village looks after them,' he smiled.

'Can you trust him? How can you be sure you get all the money he has taken?'

'I'm not sure, and I don't care as long as I have enough. Who worries if he helps himself to a bit?'

Apparently he spent the mellow winter months gently refurbishing his money-spinning fleet and travelling around seeing friends and family.

My wife and I have actually named that mind-set 'pedalos', and when people ask us what we want to do after our business consultancy, we reply 'Pedalos'. Beware! We don't mean real pedalos, because there is a good chance they don't make money anymore. No, 'pedalos' is the name of the chill-out philosophy that looks for the completely worry-free enterprise that just makes you a penny more than you can spend. Perhaps it is based somewhere that you want to be or it allows you to work the hours that enable you to pursue your passions, but in itself it is almost irrelevant what the pedalo business is because it is a means to an end. Again, if you find the idea of sunshine and leisure important to you, then you may have to shed some baggage.

The problem is that too many of us *are* our job, and we get our position in society from it. 'I am a doctor', 'I am an airline pilot', 'I am a bank manager'. You might spend your precious few weeks' holiday lying on a beach where you see a nut-brown, semi-clad person with a leather satchel full of jingling coins and a face wreathed in smiles. What status do they have? The fact that they probably earn twice as much as you do, have five times more leisure time and are a million times more happy count for nothing when you can say at a cocktail party that you are national sales director of consolidated hoo-haas and they would be forced to admit that they hire out deckchairs for a living.

People have a real challenge letting go of that, and although I most certainly don't want to get all 'new-agey, positive thinking, believe in yourself' about this, one of the benefits of business guerrillaship is that you start to exist as a person for yourself again. Well I say again, but the chances are that you have never existed for yourself before, from the day you were labelled toddler, schoolchild, student, trainee, wife, husband, manager. The Catch-22 of this, though, is that to see clearly what you want, you need to see yourself free of labels, but of course you don't become free until you start.

THERE COULD BE TROUBLE AHEAD

Maybe a bit of rest and recreation is required before you take the plunge because the most vital step is getting your head together, being realistic and thinking the whole thing through. If you don't, you could be headed for trouble. While researching this book, I became obsessed with the idea that disaster could be predicted and therefore avoided. I spent ages with a bank manager discussing why people go bust or why their venture fails.

'I know which ones are doomed when they come through the door,' she said.

'I know as soon as they put up their signs,' I agreed, 'The Happy Herb Co. and Mr Fothgill's Victorian Ironmongery says it all, but why don't you tell them?'

'I do, but they don't listen. Why don't you tell them, you're the consultant?'

'I do, but they won't listen.'

Will you listen? You bought, borrowed or nicked this book to find a few japes and wheezes on surviving out there on your own. I said I knew the recipe for disaster. Would you hear that and avoid it? Do you want to go bust? Admittedly, some bank managers are not the brightest and most sensitive people in the world, but even a railway porter can tell when a train is going to hit you simply because they have seen it before. So when the bank manager says 'Do you really want to borrow against your home for this project? I think it is doomed,' what are you thinking of when you call them an idiot and go ahead anyway? Perhaps you feel you can buck the odds, but when my future depends on something I like a racing certainty. May I suggest that one of the causes of such distortion is this personal status thing again. It is what you would be confident telling people you do at cocktail parties. Deckchair attendant or company director.

Many years ago when I was first married (above my station, a lot of people thought), my wife used to be invited to just the sort of parties to which I refer. At this time, through various shady deals, I had acquired a small fleet of lorries which I operated for, as they say, 'reward and business' (the technical description of vehicle use, as opposed to 'domestic and pleasure'). But because of my heavily chip-laden shoulders, when asked by the braying guests at these events what I did, I would answer 'I'm a removal man,' at which my poor flustered missus would leap in with 'It's his own business – he employs loads of people,' and if I was being really tricky I would rejoin 'No it isn't, no I don't.' It used to cause blazing rows but what does it matter? The trouble is that the lure of 'owning' your own business can blind you to the truth.

As we discussed earlier, self-employment in pure semantic terms means that you have elected to give yourself employment, to employ yourself. If you are your employer you must, for good business practice, give your employee (have you guessed who that is?) a job description. What job have you given yourself? When running these start-your-own-business thingys that I do, one of the perennial chestnuts is the restaurant business. Now there is nothing wrong with running a restaurant; in fact, they can be smashing gold mines, but they also have one of the most frighteningly high mortality rates among new business ventures. Some restaurateurs become millionaires, some become skint. Imagine you have decided to open a Ye Olde Tea Shoppe in the heart of some rural beauty spot. You may consider that you are now boss of a restaurant, an entrepreneur in the comestible division of the tourist boom. What you have actually done is given yourself a job as a waiter or waitress with no Sundays off ever. Did you want to work as a waiter? If you did, you would probably be better off working in someone else's restaurant where you could insist on decent pay, days off, and have no worries about borrowed money and the general economic welfare of the enterprise. Almost every small business that you could be proud to say you own, or started, has some very much less glamorous job of work attached to it, and before you start your great adventure, write a job description with a list of the duties and responsibilities, just to be sure you still want to do it. After all, if you do listen to advice, work intelligently and plan carefully, you will succeed, which may mean that you could be a waiter or waitress for the rest of your life, probably not the future you had intended. I nearly said 'planned', but if you plan your future, you would have a very clear idea of what you would like to be doing for the rest of your life.

9-TO-5 GYPSIES

Another tale that illustrates what this somewhat upside-down thinking can do for you concerns a person I used to do business with. When I had a proper day job, one of our companies used to buy salvage, and a regular supplier of some of the choicest material was a man named 'Sniffer', so-named because of his ability to sniff out a bargain. I liked to visit our suppliers so one day I climbed into the cab of one of our trucks which was going to pick up from Sniffer. We arrived in a higgledy-piggledy yard, somewhere in the middle of the country, where we were met by what I can only describe as a typical gypsy type. In fact, one could almost say a caricature gypsy type with his flat hat, leather waistcoat and colourful neckerchief. While he and my driver bargained fiercely over the weight and value of his load, I looked around his yard which was full of agricultural implements, scrap metal and bits of semi-antiques. When the deal was finally struck, he took the handful of bank notes that he received and added them to a huge roll of cash that he took from his pocket.

A rough but lucrative life, you might say, but this story has a sting in the tale. Some time later, a quirk of fate landed me at a Civic Ball, and as the guests arrived in their finery, a couple alighted from a subtle but new Mercedes Benz. The man was exquisitely groomed in carefully tailored evening dress, and despite everybody calling him 'Adrian', I thought I knew him by a different name. Then with horror I realized I did, and that I was looking at Sniffer. I buttonholed him and he seemed deeply embarrassed at being rumbled. He was no gypsy, just the reverse; he was a sophisticated, highly educated bon viveur with extravagant tastes. He had a five-bedroomed country home, and all his four children were being educated at the finest schools.

He explained that with his degree in economics he had clawed his way up the management ladder to reach somewhere about the middle in his mid-30s, where he could see he was stuck or, even worse, on the way down. He could also see that his salary could never satisfy his extravagant tastes. During this time the company he worked for as a sort of potty management training thing lent out their spare executives for worthy causes, and it was his fate to research the lot of itinerant families. Rather than educating them, they educated him. He could hardly believe the money they could knock up by their free and easy wheeler dealing. The problem was that, although the money was good, beyond his wildest expectations, he didn't fancy living in a caravan in a lay-by. Then he reached his brilliant conclusion. He would become a 9-to-5 gypsy.

He would get out of bed in his elegant home, slip on his silk dressing gown and enjoy a light continental breakfast while perusing the *Financial Times* to check on his investments. When the clock reached 8.50 a.m., he donned the moleskin trousers, steel boots et al., and strolled to his multi-vehicle garage where he would pause to flick a speck of dust off the Mercedes before walking around it to climb into the cab of his battered truck and set off to the yard. Again, another person who had successfully discovered themselves and realized that you are you and not your job.

This parallel dimension thing works just as much the other way, and as I write this book, I am battling to understand what you may call the real world. My wife leaps in to save me when people at parties come up to me and say 'What do you do, Geoff?' I reply, 'I don't know. I live and breathe.' We don't understand each other – I am not what I do. A company director with whom I worked a lot and had grown to like, once asked me in some bewilderment: 'What motivates you, Geoff?' and I could not answer him. It is going to be difficult, therefore, as we work together to get you up and running, to know what the goal should be. Let me suggest this. I would wish you to tell me in a few years time that you had a 'Really nice life'. You alone will know what will make it nice for you. Maybe, like Sniffer, you will need a pile of cash; perhaps a chance to make a living doing what you love doing, be it playing the piano, making model aeroplanes or working with children; what about the free time and sunshine that the pedalo philosophy can give? But to quote our American downshifting friend mentioned earlier, 'Make a living, don't make a dying'. I know what will not make it nice: unpayable debts, worry, being tied down and regretting ever having started. That is the downside, and if you are prepared to listen, you can be guaranteed to avoid it.

POINTS TO PONDER

1 Calculate how much your job really costs you financially and emotionally.

2 Think of the miller. He is what he does. He is not the CEO of Village Flour Inc. He is the miller, whatever the bank wants to call him.

3 Got a good business idea? Assume it stinks like a rodent.

4 If someone *does* say your idea stinks, you may have to consider the unacceptable prospect that they could be right.

5 If all your friends say it's a great idea, don't believe them. Even the bank may lend on a crap idea, after all, it's your possessions that they'll flog to get their money back.

6 Be depressingly pessimistic now rather than later. Face the truth.

7 Optimistic road maps will have you over a cliff.

8 Know for certain why you are doing this. (Yes, to pay the bills is the cool answer. Just learn that when they're paid, you can take things a bit easier, or you have to ask the question 'why?' again.)

9 If it will make you truly happy, do it or buy it, but if you've got something to prove, forget it.

10 You're the boss. You employ yourself. So what job have you just given yourself? (Did you want to be a waiter or waitress?) Write yourself a job description.

11 If it is not important to you, a rough, unpleasant job that others won't do can give you a good life out of hours.

12 If you go in with your eyes open and you are brutally realistic about your chances, you can virtually be assured of a good life.

3

Money Troubles

Well, that's the philosophical bit, so now let's just roll up our sleeves and get on with the practical aspects of Go-It-Aloning. It sometimes amazes me how some people make ends meet. Accepted, this was never intended to be a grow-rich-and-make-all-your-dreams-come-true sort of book, but sometimes I feel things just don't add up. For instance, at the time of writing this book, there are driving instructors who still charge £10 per hour. Now if you work with a benchmark of 40 hours a week, that gives a gross take-home pay of £400 per week. Before the little gear wheels in your head start revolving to calculate a yearly income of £20,000, and before you consider that you may totter by on 20 grand, think about the following. Out of that money comes the cost of running a newish car, all the surrounding bits and bobs like phone bills, advertising, stationery and so on, plus the fact that when you charge dozens of different people by the hour, it is very hard to get the hours to stand end to end.

Although I know nothing about driving schools and just pulled this example from the air, I would be surprised if the driving instructor was able to keep half the gross amount. In anybody's book, this is a fairly dismal income. Maybe some driving schools charge twice that amount, but that is just double dismal. Even with the sales and marketing skills that this book is about to give you, it is hard to charge much more than the competition and still stay in business. This is not a counselling session against the idea of becoming a driving instructor, but it is intended to steer your financial thinking towards the economics of the parallel universe that is Go It Aloning.

WHAT'S MONEY

It's time to don our kaftans, light a joss stick or two and all chant 'ommmmm' while I slip back into hippy, West-coast mode. In Chapter 2 we examined the issue of life energy and the finite amount that we are given, and it was also shown that if things are valued in life-energy terms, they can seem very expensive, but of course the converse applies as well. What is money? If you look at it as a sort of battery, it is a value store or a life-energy store. In other words, money is just a temporary place to store the value of your life energy until you want to use it, usually in exchange for the produce of someone else's life energy. Therefore, if a car worker takes 800 hours to build a car, and you value yourself at less than the hourly rate of a car worker, it will take you more than 800 hours of labour to buy one. If we catapult ourselves from hippy to Scrooge mind-set, it then stands to reason that we should put the highest possible value on our time. If you could earn 100 times what a car worker does, it will take 8 hours to buy a car.

The question I must ask you is why do you undervalue yourself? I think maybe the newly self-employed get mixed up between their previous net salary and the gross amount needed to keep things together as a Go-It-Aloner. Where £10 per hour may not seem that awful as a salary, it is pretty terrifying as a turnover. Particularly when in the early days you may have the odd week with no work. Don't panic, though, because we are going to investigate how you can multiply your value, but a good place to start is in choosing the correct enterprise.

Apart from the lack of cash, the driving lessons represent the ideal business by the Go-It-Aloner rules of measurement. Let's set aside the money thing for a moment, and consider those rules of measurement. Firstly, it is a cash business. We won't spend much time on the cash-flow bit because there are a million books dedicated to the subject, but suffice to say it can be a bit of a shocker if you don't get paid. A lot of you will be considering consultancy, so the fees are about as near as you are going to get to a normal salary. It is not unusual, however, even when dealing with large corporate clients, to wait 90 days or more for your money. It is not quite so bad if that cash is rock solid guaranteed, like when you have a purchase order or goods satisfaction note, but you still have to live while you are waiting, and some clients never pay.

I have developed a bit of a nose for it now. Recently I was invited with a colleague to visit a thrusting new high-tech company. When I saw the car-park full of new Mercedes, the piddling cherub fountain in the foyer along with the 25-year-old Armani-clad directors, I knew. I whispered to my chum, 'That's it, we won't get paid.' He knows me for the happy-go-lucky character that I'm not, and he shot me a deadly glance for endangering this fine new client. Studiously ignoring him, I demanded money up front, and after a lot of toing and froing, we finally got a third of our fee. At the liquidation hearing, I was told that we were the only people to have been paid anything. My colleague, instead of shedding tears of gratitude and offering me a lavish lunch, got all tetchy about me crowing 'told you so'.

THROW A TV IN THE DUMP

Money up front is a bit of a policy thing with me. Again, it boils down to what money is. I won't bore you with what my business turns over, but I suppose it is just about enough, so everyone was amused at the wobbly I threw when a company went down owing me £150. In percentage terms my business could take the loss, and in time, so could yours, but don't be so sanguine because it is your very own money that just got lost. I had toyed with the idea of treating myself to a portable television, but as it was a tightish month, I took the sensible decision not to buy it. Then this pillock took to the hills with my, and a lot of other people's, money. For £150 I could have bought the television and chucked it in a skip, which would have given me more pleasure than never getting it at all.

I worked in advertising many years ago, and one of my mentors in this jungle of self-employment was a buccaneer of the marketing world. I ended up trailing around with this guy for a few months, and whilst I learnt nothing about advertising because he was a klutz when it came to creativity, I learnt a lot about getting the cash. We would visit potential clients and I would do all the flash magic-marker creative stuff. When we had finished the client would say, almost out of politeness, 'Where do we go from here?' My colleague's reply was almost literally, 'Well, to start with, you must hand me a wad of cash.' He had this thing he called the 'concept fee'. A great number of marketing people take a brief from the client, and then do a large amount of unpaid speculative work which they present as a 'pitch' in the hope of winning the work, but not our friend. He would ask for a few hundred pounds to cover the expense of this 'pitch'.

The obvious argument against this is that the potential client won't pay, and will have security hurl you into the street. This is a valid argument, particularly when all the competition work for nothing, but it did have some merit because when he did succeed (which was surprisingly often), there was a sort of double whammy. The first was that after he secured the 'concept fee', it didn't really matter if the job went ahead or not because he could make a handsome living out of concept fees alone. The second, however, tended to mean that the customer, having spent the money with him and not with the others, felt that if they didn't go ahead with him, part of the budget was lost. In other words, if you can get money up front, in stage payments or deposits, the work is far more likely to go ahead. I am not suggesting that you should conduct your business the way this old rogue did, but is to illustrate a point.

THE FIRST THREE RATS GO FREE OFFER

To return to the Pied Piper, see how much better it would have been if he had got money in advance. He could have enticed a sample batch of rats away and taken the money up front.

Another side-effect of this is that people who have paid tend to be more satisfied than people who haven't. As we will see when we get to the selling bit, people can be convinced of anything, especially when they are allowed to convince themselves.

The problem arises when this phenomenon runs out of control. If someone has failed to pay and you press them, they will often make up excuses about the quality of your product or service: 'My guests were disappointed with the temperature of the soup you provided', 'The valences seem a bit wrinkly', 'One leg is shorter than the other'. You will think to yourself that they are just inventing problems to avoid paying, and at first you may be right, but after a while they start to believe their own propaganda. This can mean that, even when they do get the money to pay you, they are reluctant to do so, and you will get into the mire of knocking money off to get a settlement, and other indignities. Not only that, because the customer now believes their own propaganda, they will not be satisfied and will become a bad ambassador for you. After all, if you have just sued the shirt off someone, they are hardly likely to recommend you to their chums.

If, on the other hand, you get the money out of them up front, the king's new clothes syndrome comes into play. Someone who has already spent huge wads of moolah will tend to justify the expenditure and tell everyone what a good deal they had. Now you have the first benchmark against which to measure your new money-spinning scheme. Is it a money-up-front business?

THE MILLSTONE AROUND YOUR NECK

Let's see what else our driving school has to offer as an example. One that immediately springs to mind is the fact that it has no premises to speak of. There may be things that you treasure or enjoy being the owner of, but if you were on a sinking ship you would be encouraged to abandon them before leaping over the side. The reason is that in the water they cease to be treasures, but become the millstone that will drag you to a watery grave. Premises, mortgages and leases can have the same effect. This is not to say that you should never have them, but remember that if things don't go quite so well as planned, they can come back and haunt you. The essence of good jungle warfare is to travel light and live off the land.

When I storm into the commercial jungle with my proverbial rucksack of baked beans, I see people with chest freezers and home ice-cream makers on their backs. With these small business start-ups, I feel like a shepherd with a flock of lambs to see through the night. I can hear the wolves howling out in the darkness and I know the laws of nature decree that some of my charges will fall victim and will not see the dawn. I am desperate to reduce this terrible attrition, but what can my individual flock members do to stop being torn limb from limb?

They say if you cut your hand and fall in the sea in Australia, the sharks can smell your blood and come circling in from as far away as Java. Well, take it from me, as soon as you say 'Let's invest some of our savings in starting our own thing', the photocopier, espresso coffee machine, office equipment, electronic till and telephone equipment salesmen can smell the fresh blood and come circling in from similarly incredible distances.

WHY GO BUST?

I become unspeakably depressed when I visit a new business and walk into an Aladdin's cave of new kit. This is your life we are discussing and it is not too good to start off by mortgaging it. Again, consider the conversation I had with the banks while researching this book. I asked quite boldly and unequivocally, 'Do your small business customers go bust?' 'Often,' came the reply.

Listen, dear reader, do you want to go bust? Do you think it is a risk worth taking, a bit of a gamble? Well, believe me, it shouldn't be. Success should be an inevitable result of careful planning. The self-employment for job security story is such a jolly jape because most people see it as a gamble, but what I am talking about is providing yourself with genuinely safe, secure employment that will pay back what you put in with a rich dividend.

Surely, then, if we can discover the hidden rocks together, it would make sense to steer around them.

> 'So, if you suspect they are going to go bust, why do you lend them money?' I asked the banks.
> 'Well, if we do suspect that, we don't,' comes the reply, 'but then not everybody is honest about what they already owe or their level of sales.'

This is the voice of an honest bank manager because, rest assured, it is most unlikely that the banks would wish to lend money on an unsecured basis. In other words, they will require security against your home, or some other form of iron-clad guarantee.

The cynic might say that a less than scrupulous bank manager might lend money to you even if he knows the enterprise is doomed because he cannot lose. You pull off the million-to-one shot, and you thank him for his support. Cock it up and he has your house. Bear in mind how banks make money: they make their money make a profit. For example, you borrow £10,000, you pay back maybe £12,000 in a year's time. This is if you fail or not. If your dream lies in ashes at your feet, they don't just show up and skin you for the £10,000. Oh no. They have you for the full £12,000. Unlike any other business I know, they make money whether their customers go bust or not.

The first point, I suppose, is that if you are flush with cash, forget that little tavern and open a bank. The second and probably most important is that you must be convinced that you can earn money faster and more efficiently than the bank because this makes the difference between life and death. It isn't just small businesses that suffer from this, because it is the key to the very immoral but lucrative pastime of asset stripping. You find yourself a nice chain of shoe shops or whatever, making around £2 million a year profit in a good year, and you pay £20 million for it. Shut it down and flog its 200 branches for £½ a million each. I leave the rest of the maths for your entertainment, but it is clear that the shops are worth more dead than alive. Perhaps it was a bit of asset stripping that got you on the trail of self-employment.

The moral is to be very careful about capital employed in your enterprise. The posh City-speak description of the mess you can get yourself in is 'overgearing'. Remember the bank has spent a few hundred years working out how best to make money. This could well be your first attempt so please don't be too sure that you are necessarily better at making money than they are, because you only keep the difference. You could make £2,001 on £10,000 employed (and borrowed), pay the bank £2,000, and keep a pound for yourself. This may keep you alive long enough to continue, in effect, to work not for yourself but for the bank.

Are banks such cruel, heartless, money-grabbing animals? In a lot of cases, they are not, and when my potential entrepreneurial stars complain about the treatment they receive at the hands of the bank, it is because they won't lend, not because they will. If a bank turns down your loan application for this fail-safe scheme of yours, they might just have a reason.

BEWARE OF SMILING BANK MANAGERS BEARING GIFTS

The biggest whinges I get are from people who say that their bank won't lend them money, and the second biggest is the story of what the bank did to them when they went bust. People joke that a bank is a company that lends umbrellas when it's not raining. There's some truth, perhaps, in that, but to be fair, if it was my business to lend umbrellas I wouldn't lend one to a person plunging over a cliff in flames. OK, it may slow the descent a little, but it only marginally delays the inevitable, and I would have lost my umbrella which is my business.

If the banks won't lend you money, are they mean, cruel and jealous of your success or are they too stupid to see the brilliance of your cunning plan? Look, I am not over-fond of banks myself, but they should be looked upon as kind of neutral. Bear in mind that they are in business to make money by lending more. Rest assured, if they thought you were certain to succeed they would rush to lend. Of course, the irony is that they can only really be sure of your success after you succeed. Then they want to lend you money. Hence the umbrella story.

If we can digress for just a moment, there is quite a sinister threat lurking here for you. As we said early on, we get all bitter and resentful when the bank is 'too stupid' to lend us money, but the opposite can happen. You can make a huge success of things and the bank tells you that you are a genius. What perceptive, clever people they are to have spotted that certain truth; therefore they must be right about everything else. From the bank's point of view, they see you as a good bet, but be warned: they have a strange way of working this out. They don't judge you on the warm relationship they have built with you because you are a good and special human being. They do it through a formula and statistics, the sort of formula that calculates that a ball bounces forever because it did the last 23 times, or that as most people die in bed, beds are very dangerous and should be avoided at all costs.

Now listen, you have made a few quid; you have now proved that you are probably brighter than the people at the bank. After all, if they were so darn clever, they wouldn't be working at the bank but would be out with you, making their own way in the world. You believed this when they turned you down, so why not believe it now? They will want to lend money to you at an inappropriate time. You will see over the next few chapters that the secret of success is being able to sell yourself to the right people. Don't you think the banks know this? If they think you are a good bet, they want to 'sell' you money. The clever bit about selling is that the seller decides when the intended victim will buy, and the subtle thing about buying is buying exactly when you want to. Just because they say you are a genius has not improved their business acumen, and if you let them suck you in, you could be making fatal mistakes.

A CAUTIONARY TALE

A great chum of mine built his business up to a point where it moved well outside the parameters of this book and became a small but pukka company. From the start, the bank and suppliers were less than friendly, particularly the biggest supplier of raw materials to his industry. He was persistently treated like a second-class citizen by them, and when he visited them, the management would treat him like dirt, not a customer. Why did he tolerate it? He had to. They really were the only supplier of the components he needed.

As his business expanded, however, his supplier was hitting rock bottom, and the whole industry was shattered to hear that the receivers had been called in. My chum had done so well that he had amassed a nice stash of cash, and on chatting to the receiver, he was surprised to find that with some modest borrowing he could buy his old enemy, lock stock and barrel. He would need the bank's support after the event, but their involvement would be nominal and should not have caused a problem. He bought, and did the thing we all can only dream of. Putting on his roughest working clothes, he walked into the head office of his new acquisition, straight into the managing director's lair. His old tormentor, who didn't know who the new owner of his company was, blustered with fury at the rough oik who had invaded his space. 'How dare you come in here! Who the hell do you think you are?' 'I am your new boss, and you are sacked,' grinned our chum.

This should have been the happy ending, but now the trouble started. Our hero had already found a buyer for the firm, its equipment and stock, and an impressive head office in London with a large plot of land. As it was at the height of the property boom, the price would have financed the whole deal and made some extra. But no, the bank said he was wrong to sell on the existing market. If he developed the site himself, he would make money beyond the dreams of avarice. The figures worked something like, if he borrowed £10 million – yep, that's right, £10 million – to develop the site he could sell for a minimum of £25 million. Things didn't work quite as quickly as they should. A year had passed while planning consent was obtained, and as no income was received, the bank account rose by £2 million. Of course, it is easy to bandy figures about like that in a book, but bear in mind that £2 million is enough money for you to live in comfort for the rest of your life and some, and he had just had that added to his overdraft.

The rest is predictable. The property market collapsed, the bank took all the assets to cover the loan, plus his original company which continued to be successful. It was sold to one of my friend's most hated competitors. In the final year, our friend had to die the death of a thousand cuts as the bank bounced cheques, put the company into administration and ran the accounts at punitive interest rates.

If you are a successful chocolate maker, then you are not a property speculator, and nor is your bank. I know you are a genius, but don't let weasel words cloud your judgement. Really, it is better to regret the business risks you didn't take rather than the ones you did, but let's get back on course. You are angry at the bank for not lending you money, but that is their business. They even publish a book on starting your own business, for heaven's sake. That is a bit like the McDonald's guide to vegetarian cooking, so beware of books published by people with an axe to grind. Read them, but remember who published them.

POINTS TO PONDER

1 Do your sums – charge enough and don't forget your overheads (I'll show you how to sell that higher price later).
2 Make sure you get paid.
3 Better still, get the money up front. If your clients are touchy about it, my experience says they are often the ones who wouldn't have paid anyway.
4 Customers who don't pay soon believe they shouldn't pay, then you've got trouble.
5 Travel light, and don't sign up for anything you don't really have to.
6 If the bank won't lend to you, they may be right not to. Do you really, hand on your heart, promise you know

finance better than the bank does? You had better be right – your life depends on it!

7 If the bank *wants* to lend you money, you could be in even bigger trouble.

4

Swimming with the Sharks

Why won't the banks lend to you? Do they know something you don't? I asked my bank manager again if he could spot trouble coming. He replied that he was only human (I would have said barely), and marginal cases were in the lap of the gods, but he could be sure of the real sure-fire failures. Those total clunkers. Is your idea a total clunker?

I really want to be your chum, and the best way not to be is to tell you your idea stinks, but if it does, surely it must be best to know now. Let me suggest, then, that without rancour, and by looking at the opinion and experience of others, we find the true recipe for disaster.

I asked my bank manager if he still lends to the ones that he knows are unlikely to succeed. 'Sometimes,' he replied. You may brand him an unfeeling animal for lending to people with little hope, but it is not that simple. People are often in that grey area of 'will they, won't they?' and worse still, if they are convinced of the validity of their scheme, they will source their finance from even more unsympathetic areas. My wife and I play a sinister game which I assure you gives me little pleasure. As we take our daily stroll, we see new businesses that have sprung up: 'Shirt 'n' Collars', 'China Animals for All', 'Tupper's Tasty Tea Emporium', and I turn to my missus and whisper: 'Doomed.' You understand that this is a prediction not a curse, but sadly and inevitably a very accurate prediction.

THE WRONG SUMS

So how is it that the bank manager and I know when a business is doomed to failure, but the owner does not? Firstly, we must consider this business of cash. Most people start their new life with oodles of enthusiasm and optimism. The problem is that there is no more explosive formula than a mixture of enthusiasm, optimism and cash. Optimism will tell you that if you buy them for £10, you will sell them for £20. Do that a mere three times an hour and you make a minimum of £30 an hour. Enthusiasm will tell you that at the start you won't mind working 10 or even 12 hours a day, six days a week, just to get a flying start at that overdraft.

A TALE TO TERRIFY

Picture the scene. After a lifetime of drudgery at International Thingy Plungers, you are free. You can burn those business suits, park the company Ford in the canal and say bye-bye to the rush hour. You find that funny old shop down a quaint but forgotten back street. The cheery old gentleman who opens the creaky door wears fingerless gloves and pince-nez spectacles. When you ask him how much he would rent the shop to you for, he laughs with a tinkling chuckle and his old eyes sparkle with forgotten joy. He loves to see people making a new start, and he tells you that by OKing a simple agreement you can move in for nothing until you get settled, and then as you get on, perhaps you would share just a little of your success with him.

Let's just stop here and look more closely at the scenario. Why, for instance, does the sweet old gentleman carry a posh organizer and Jaguar key ring, and why does this erstwhile Santa wear Gucci shoes? Because, dear reader, he is a commercial estate agent and he has just stitched you into a 25-year full-repairing lease on their real lemon property, the ramshackle tip in an area where the kids can remove car wheels at a speed that would shame a Formula One team. All that he had to tempt your poor eyes with was a measly rent-free period. Oh, I did say full-repairing lease didn't I? Well, I am no legal expert, but may I suggest that full-repairing means that you do all the repairs? Seems fair?

You have set out on a new journey and you have things to learn, and you certainly will be very different people in a year or two. I hope very successful, but undoubtedly different. The business may be bigger, smaller, or just plain different, so why sign a 25-year lease that can come back to haunt you long after you have changed or even stopped the business? There are true horror stories of people who have sold their businesses and assigned the lease. Twenty years later, the massive investment company that owns the freehold shows up and demands 18 years of back rent you are liable for because the tenant has done a bunk. For the facts of this, it is best to see a solicitor, although beware – we are in bank manager territory here. Remember, this guy is not necessarily your friend, and even more important, he is probably no great entrepreneur. Go to him, negotiate a pre-price deal so he doesn't stitch you up, and get an hour or so of his time on the subject you want to discuss – in this case, leases and property law.

THE VULTURES GATHER

OK, so you go ahead and rent the old shop. A passer-by would see lights burning late into the night as the two of you, dressed in old jeans and T-shirts, work and laugh like newlyweds, cobwebs in your hair and paint specks on your faces. As you stand back, arms around each other, paint brushes held slackly by your sides to admire your handy work, a cheery head pops around the door, despite the late hour. Laughing eyes twinkle beneath a mop of tousled hair and above a ready smile. He tells you what a great job you have done and hopes that you won't be offended that he just had to stop and tell you in person. He gasps in respect and awe when he hears that you are to open Grimsville Estates' first Aromatic Herb Emporium. He just knows that you are going to do well and maybe, just maybe, he can help.

Although he knows that aromatic herbs will be the coming thing on the Grimsville, there is, he tells you, also a very strange lack of anywhere to get a photocopy. There has been a wailing and a gnashing of teeth on the Grimsville for want of photocopying facilities for a long time. He counsels you not to be greedy and tempted to profiteer from this golden opportunity, but to offer photocopies at virtually a community service price of 10p each. After all, you would be putting something back into the area, the machine would attract people to sample the aromatic herbs, and at a modest estimate of 1,000 daily copies, the unit would earn a well-deserved £100 a day. Where could you get such a wondrous device you ask, and surely they are very expensive?

His infectious laugh soon gets you chuckling along. As luck would have it, he represents a sort of charitable institution which helps small businesses who are prepared to contribute to the community. This company will give you a machine virtually free: all you have to do is pay them 3p a copy and agree to take a paltry minimum of 500 copies each week. How long does this agreement last? 'For the time being,' he smiles. 'Just OK the agreement.' DON'T. He is the devil in disguise. That is a lease he wants you to sign. Apart from the fact that no one on Grimsville is the slightest bit interested in photocopies and you will be lucky to shift five a week, the agreement you have signed will probably result in you paying £400,000 for a £5,000 machine over the 150 years the agreement runs for.

THE SPELL THAT SCARES THEM AWAY

You may be asking yourself what photocopiers have to do with you, but it is not just photocopiers. I visit these small businesses and I see the new till, the new microwave, the custom-woven and free-laundered entrance mat, the colourful easy-wash space-age plastic sun blinds, the computers and the dishwasher. Remember we mentioned what happens if you bathe with an open wound in Australia – the sharks can smell your blood in Java. Well the signing of that lease or that loan application is like those pungent, appetizing drops of blood, and in they circle, their sinister, dark, triangular fins slicing through the waves on the way to their feeding frenzy. And you, kid, are item number one on the menu.

More than sharks who are mere animals, the circling sales-men have an almost supernatural ability to smell out their vic-tims, but as in all great B-movies, there is a spell that drives them off. Like garlic for vampires and silver bullets for were-wolves, the travelling salesman is driven into crumbling, howl-ing piles of defeated dust by a simple incantation. Repeat after me: "I am sorry, but I need to think about it'. That phrase is lit-erally the death of a salesman. They fear it so much that whole books have been written on how to deal with it (I have even written one of them myself, for heaven's sake). Remember, this is no game, and even if the guy is selling equipment you need at the best possible price, say 'I need to think about it'.

ON CATCHING HUGE, POISONOUS SNAKES

If I hurled you into a room with a huge, poisonous snake in it and said 'Catch it alive', what would you do? Come on now, make your mind up. It has reared up and it is hissing at you. Come on, catch it, don't fiddle about. I would think that the chances of being bitten are high – and it makes the whole exploit far too exciting for me – but one small change can make all the difference. What if I said there was going to be a poisonous snake in there tomorrow and I would like you to take it alive? You would have a day to plan. A single paltry day that can make all the difference. I can feel the wheels in your head turning as I write: 'Strong boots, a net, some thick gloves, a long stick, a gun, some face protection, tranquillizer spray, and some expert advice.' I suggest that, after that vital day, you would stride into that room with confidence.

Do exactly the same with anyone who is trying to persuade you to do anything. For a start, the snake analogy was not acci-dental. Remember, this book is to help you achieve success by avoiding disaster. It is a recipe that doesn't welcome short cuts. Imagine you are offered the deal of a lifetime. It was your lucky day when you bumped into this person. In a reassuring voice he will say, 'Just OK the agreement, and you can start enjoying the profits from tomorrow.'

By the way, I am not accidentally repeating myself with this 'just OK the agreement' bit because this is pure sales speak which you must learn, because part of your success depends on turning you from prey to hunter. More of this later, but suffice to say for now that the above sounds better than 'Sign the contract and you can start paying for it from tomorrow.' You reply, 'I will think about it.'

THE SIRENS' SONG

Now it starts. If the salesman has been badly trained he will bluster and threaten. If he is slick he will glide into a well-oiled routine and, take my word for it, you are in real danger.

I recall the story of Odysseus who heard that the Sirens' song could, through its seductive sweetness, lure a man to his death. Because of this he filled his crew's ears with wax to stop them hearing it. Odysseus himself, however, like the big macho pillock that he was, decided that as he was going into this thing with his eyes open (or should I say ears), he would be able to resist. Mind you, his pillockness didn't stretch as far as not letting himself be tied securely to the mast of his ship, as the little craft battled valiantly through the mountainous seas, and around the vicious rocks that surrounded the Sirens' Isle. Over the crashing waves he heard snatches of sweet maidens' song. 'Catchy little number,' he mused, then within seconds he was literally mad with desire and in a frenzy that he barely survived. That should teach him to be over-confident, but it is now you who must resist the sirens' song of the salesman.

A WELL-OILED ROUTINE

These salespeople go off to seminars to learn how to deal with 'I'll think about it'. Some of the methods are considered so powerful that they have literally been patented and trademarked. That is why I am a little cautious about mentioning them by name, but be warned: the more friendly and easily it seems to be going, the bigger the danger you are in.

One method works like this. As soon as you say 'I would like to think it over,' the salesman says 'Of course, a decision as important as this should be thought about,' with which he will pack all his things and make to leave. For some bizarre reason, it makes you feel a bit of a heel for treating such a nice guy in such an offhand manner, so it is almost with relief that you find he has stopped at the door, Columbo style. Clasping his brow in obvious distress, he pleads 'Would you do me a great favour?' After being such a total turd to him, how can you refuse? 'Well, OK.' He sits back down. 'You see, I feel I have done a bad job.' He waits, perhaps with his shoulders lifting and falling as his body is wracked with silent sobs. The atmosphere grows oppressive and you say, 'No, you haven't.' Now he cries out loud, 'I have, I have, my company put together this wonderful opportunity for you and I have failed to put it across to you.' 'No, you have done a great job.' 'Really?' he asks with a little watery smile playing across his lips. He blows his nose noisily and cheers up just enough to ask, 'Then what do you need to think about? You see, when people say they have something to think about, it means there are things they are not sure of.' 'Well, I don't know, I just want to think things over,' you reply. Careful now, you are swimming cheerfully with the crocodiles, out to a place where the water is deep enough for lunch to be enjoyed.

'Why don't I make a list of those things?' he suggests. He will write numbers from 1 to 10 or even 20 down the side of a page, and will then wait, pen poised. 'What is your first concern?' he asks gently. 'Well, it is a bit too expensive for a start.' Twisting your words slightly he writes 'Price' at number one. 'Anything else?' 'It's a horrible colour.' He writes 'Colour' at number two. If you are really lucky you will think of maybe five things, with of course the most important first, and by four or five you are scraping the bottom of the barrel.

'Is that all?' he purrs reassuringly. To your embarrassment you have barely filled a quarter of the numbers available and his pen is still poised. You nod in confusion and ZIP, his pen draws a line under your paltry collection. 'These are your objections with going ahead?' 'Well, yes.' 'If I could satisfactorily deal with each of these, then you would have no more worries and you could proceed, correct?' 'Well yes.' 'OK, the first, price.'

Rest assured, he won't cut the price, but starts asking if you enjoy a nice cup of tea, and if so, how many cups you drink each day. He then tells you that the cost of his lease is less than the price of a cup of tea a day. 'Surely the peace of mind a quality security system can bring is worth the price of a cup of tea, don't you agree?' 'Yes.' The pen strikes out number one.

Now you can see it coming. If we tie you to the mast, will you resist it? Please believe me, I am not being rude when I suggest that you are an easy (well easier) victim. These tricks have long since stopped working on commercial buyers (that is why you will notice I don't make too much fuss of them in the selling bit of this book). The reason is that the commercial buyer is buying for the satisfaction of others. In other words, the consequences of a buying cock-up could be fatal in career terms. He is cautious because of the consequences, but you have no one to answer to but yourself. So there is no one to go back to but yourself, and thus you can make instant and highly regrettable decisions. After all, we agreed you won't fire yourself – bankrupt yourself maybe – but never fire yourself. Perhaps you should pre-arrange some consequences. You could lay a large lump hammer on your back doorstep and swear a solemn oath that if you buy on the day, good or bad, you will beat your thumbnail black with the lump hammer. After a day you can do as you please and your nail is safe. Watch with pleasure as the salesperson screams in agony at statements like, 'Only a penny per copy? What a bargain. Pop back tomorrow, and if my solicitor has vetted and approved this contract as being good for me, I will sign it.'

Don't take any rubbish about 'I can't keep this offer open after today.' If you take the advice of this book, sure, you may miss some bargains, but I bet they have a ratio of about 1 to 100 to the stitch-ups you will have avoided. Take contracts to solicitors or, even cheaper, to the other guy's competitor. They will pick holes in his deal: after all, they want to eat you themselves. Ask friends, ask enemies, sit by the fire and ruminate. Make me happy when I eavesdrop your conversation and hear you say 'I am glad we didn't buy that grindle plunger.'

A little aside here. The salesman was, for the sake of expedience, masculine, but beware the female of the species who can be, to quote a cliché, 'deadlier than the male'. Men can easily slip into macho pushiness but not that seemingly simple-minded bubbly little blonde who just popped back because she must have 'left her car keys'. 'By the way,' she says, 'do you understand where you are supposed to sign this thing, because I don't?' (chuckle). All this masks a mind like a stiletto and an appetite for your blood that puts her male colleagues in the shade.

OR WORSE STILL, THE BANK MANAGER MIGHT BE RIGHT

Are these small enterprises doomed simply because they fell prey to the prowling salespeople who fed off them, or are they fed off because they are already wounded and make an easy meal for the cruising shoal?

Let's go from the point where not even the bank manager is nasty enough to make money out of you, and turns down your loan application. This means that, in the bank's eyes, your idea is one of the ones that is unlikely to succeed. Remember the bank manager I spoke to? He couldn't guarantee that the good ones would succeed, and sometimes those in the grey area surprised him, but he could be almost certain of the disasters. I need you to succeed, I must encourage you to succeed, and I know that you have got all sniffy because the bank manager won't back your excellent scheme. I am sure that I am aggravating you even more by suggesting that he might be right.

Before storming off to teach the world a lesson by showing us how it is done, let's examine the situation and put matters right to the point where things will proceed smoothly. First, is your idea a non-starter? If it is, we have got trouble, so for the moment let's see what has upset our financiers.

HE EVEN LAUGHED AT MY CUNNING PLANS

It happened to me 12 million years ago, when I left my day job to set up my training consultancy. I hadn't come away with much so the business had to be started on a shoestring. A down payment on a one-room backstreet office, my living wage for six months, some cheap office furniture, a small but respectable and reliable car, stationery, a computer and a part-timer just to do my letters and what not. This all came to around £10,000, about three times that at today's money, but nonetheless a modest sum with which to found a business dynasty.

The bank manager was still wiping away the tears of laughter as he escorted me to the door. 'OK, then,' I asked him, 'What are you prepared to lend me?' After a short but vigorous scuffle which resulted in security hurling me into the street, I discovered the answer to be 'Nothing.'

Now if you find yourself in this position, there is a very dangerous route you can take. If you have been reading American self-help books, you will pick yourself up, brush the dust off, look the world straight in the eye, and say to yourself something stupid like 'It is not the man who is knocked down who is beat, but the one who stays down'. Listen, if someone has just beaten the crap out of me, I am not going to get up and let them do it again. I lie in a darkened room for a few days, whimpering softly and feeling sorry for myself, as I did after the bank debacle. It was the saving of me and will be of you, so get all your positive-thinking books and burn them. Repeat to yourself my recommended self-motivation phrase, 'Life is just a bowl of toenails' and you won't go wrong. It is always the optimist who says 'Behind the next door lies opportunity' and the pessimist who says 'Behind the next door lies a blood-crazed nightmare terror beast that is dying to sink its flesh-rending fangs into my helpless body'. Let me tell you that you won't find a pessimist's entrails splashed up the wall. Maybe you have to go through life's doors, but at least you can do it carefully. The nightmare terror beast that awaits you in this instance is the temptation to find finance elsewhere.

A TEMPTING OFFER YOU SHOULD REFUSE

Oh, please be careful. It is all too easy. Those awful salespeople we talked about earlier are only too eager to help you get the things 'you need'. Every garage paints, in jolly colours, the fact that you can have the car or van you need for only £99 a month. The office (perhaps a little larger than you needed but then there is room to expand) is rent-free for a while, the copier is free, just 3p per copy, and all the furniture and even your business clothes can be leased.

If you think that banks can make money out of money, they haven't got anything on the leasing companies, who are, as it happens, often owned by the banks. They have cheery and clever methods of hiding the ways they make money out of you, but rest assured: if you start your enterprise out of leased kit, you are heavily loaded from the word go.

Even with vehicles at interest-free rates, or the just-buy-50-per-cent deals, they make their money somewhere. The interest-free car can probably be bought elsewhere for a 16-per-cent or more discount, and 50-per-cent deals really make me laugh. The impression you are given is that you own half of the vehicle and that the manufacturer owns the other half. If it is a £20,000 car, you give them ten grand, and they stand the rest until you can afford it, but it is like the old half a dog joke: they get the end that wags the tail, and you get the end that bites. Or, in their terms, you get the bit that rusts and depreciates, and they get the half that is still worth half the value of the original car. I bet you would like a car that depreciates not a penny, then ask them if you can swap halves. I bet they leap at the idea.

DON'T TRY BLACKCURRANT PICKING

Here you sit with all these brand-new things and all these lease agreements. Maybe disaster isn't assured, but it is a bit like sitting in a birch-bark canoe with an anvil chained around your neck. You can't afford too much rocking about or rapids, or even the occasional hole, because the end will be swift and catastrophic.

You say you have done your sums, but we have all done our sums. The problem about doing sums was brought home to me when I was a kid and saw an advert for blackcurrant pickers. They were paying 50p a bucket at a time when £10 per week was good money. There had to be a catch so I did my sums and my first research. I attacked my mum's blackcurrant bushes with gusto, a pair of scissors and a bucket. It was full in less than five minutes. I thought that, with practice, I could get even faster, but I erred on the side of caution, basing the experimental time on 15 minutes a bucket, that was £2 per hour, and £20 per day. The price of a new bike every day.

When I arrived, the 'bucket' was like a 40-gallon oil drum, the currants were on bushes two feet high so you had to work on your hands and knees in clothes-ruining mud, and you were penalized if the bushes were damaged. After a back-breaking day, I presented a one-third-full bucket. The man explained that, although the currants were going to make jam, he didn't want the process started in the bucket, particularly when there was a liberal helping of mud included. The upshot was that he refused to pay even for that sad offering, but what a golden lesson I learned about sums. They may give you an idea of your potential, but I think you can never be pessimistic enough.

Remember, this book is a survival guide and we started off modelling ourselves on guerrillas or post-apocalypse survivalists, and their number-one rule is TRAVEL LIGHT. The Japanese army conquered Asia on bicycles and it wasn't until we abandoned our jungle-bogged tanks and took to mules that we fought them off.

BACK TO THE DARKENED ROOM

The last time you left me, I was lying in my darkened room after the kicking I received from the bank. What did I do next and how can it help you?

Many of you reading this book may wish to apply the skills you used when you had a 'proper day job'. Perhaps you were a human resources director, a lift service engineer or head of catering. I see the mistake I started to make, but was not allowed to through the bank's intransigence, repeated over and over again by the new Go-It-Aloners. Just because you have set up as a consultant or what not in your old skill doesn't mean that you need to re-create your old working environment in every detail.

We visit an office in a smoked glass palace, and there is a shining new brass plate with 'The Laughing Vole Engineering Consultancy Partnership' emblazoned on it. I am not knocking other people's enterprises (well, perhaps I am), but I am a bit nervous of these serviced small-business-centre type offices. Without being derogatory on a subject I don't know too much about, they must have done their sums and come up with a 50-room building that costs them £1000 per week, with a rent of £100 per room. Again I leave the sums to you, but their sell is on the lavish shared facilities. You see the oak-panelled board room, the international electronic communications centre, and the beautiful but efficient receptionists who will represent your company.

Please do not let your dreams stand in the way of survival. When you fantasize about hosting high-powered top-level meetings in that panelled room while your royal decrees are flashed across the globe bringing long-reaching ramifications from Tokyo to New York, just remember the kid who thought he could buy a bike from one day's fruit picking. Examine all the charges – there is nothing that in one way or another you won't be paying for. Fair price or not, let me assure you to start with that you don't need any of it yet.

I'd also like to offer a personal word of warning. My experience suggests that these service offices don't give a great impression because they are often quite flash but very easy to rent short term. This means that they can attract the fly boys. In other words, renting such an office can be tantamount to trading off the back of a suitcase in Oxford Street. So instead of giving that executive feel to your enterprise as intended, it could blight it.

I am not, of course, talking about small workshops or communal workspaces. If you have a physical trade that requires space, then you may have to rent that space, and often local councils or the Training and Enterprise Council (TEC) will provide subsidized space. This is great.

Another thing I saw was a huge old dockside warehouse that was devoted to freelancers of one industry, in this case, advertising. The landlord literally chalked out your area on the floor, as large as you needed or could afford. The illustrators used the copywriters, who used the typesetters, who used the illustrators, plus the clients used it as a sort of open market to source the services they needed. The other bonus of such as scheme is that it stops you being lonely, which can be a bit of a thing to start with.

THE CURSE OF THE HAT STAND

When we enter the office of the 'Laughing Vole Engineering Consultancy', it is a showcase of modern equipment. The tower PC flickers purposefully on its own limed-oak fitment, while the 46-colour laser printer awaits, similarly accommodated. There is a fax, the mobile phone, the three-line switchboard, desks, filing cabinets, and even a hat stand. Perhaps the founders of the company re-created the office environment they had just left in a sort of comfort gesture, so that they felt they were still 'going to work'.

Your life depends on your future success. Before deciding to Go It Alone, you discuss strategy with your closest confidante. After writing that incisive cash-flow forecast, you make the break from your old life and go out and buy ... a hat stand. I know you had all of these things in your old job. If the company you were in was big enough, I wouldn't be surprised if there was a 'hat stand procurement officer' on 24-hour call. Perhaps self-employment hasn't been your life's ambition and you got washed up on my shore after the typhoon and shipwreck of redundancy.

Why were you made redundant? Probably because your old firm was losing money. When large firms or organizations lose money, they seem to do it in breathtaking amounts. You hear on the news that Consolidated Knot Holes put out a profit warning after announcing losses of £400 million last year. They lost their money, you lost your job, and somewhere there is a vast warehouse full of unwanted hat stands. If you were a service engineer, every couple of years you would get a shiny new van, those special tools, and a lavish selection of spares. Sadly, the well-equipped engineer needs these things, but we just can't afford them yet so we must manage without.

This is the first day of your new life and there is no point whatsoever in re-creating your old working environment. If you are worried about your status, I can save you face by using a marvellous bit of 21st-century business-speak gobbledygook, and help you to create (to quote every modern guru from Handy to Peters) the virtual office. That is what I did when I was finally coaxed out of my darkened room. I created a virtual office. I had virtually got an office – one that existed in Cyberspace – but in fact it was my back bedroom. I even organized a virtual executive saloon car – in Cyberspace it was a Jag but in the flesh it bore a passing resemblance to an elderly van that a compassionate chum had given me. All that was needed was to casually toss down the Jag key ring at client meetings, after secreting the offensive but reliable heap about four blocks away, and bingo, virtual executive transport.

The virtual office was substantially challenged when a client absolutely insisted on meeting in my office. A rather nice brass plate was made up which I still have, and was fastened by sticky pads on the main door of a much wealthier chum who lent me his office and all his staff for a large bottle of malt whisky. This is, of course, seat of the pants stuff, but there are ways and means of obtaining a smart mile-eating car, a very upmarket meeting place and all the office service you need, quite above board and legitimately, without tying that millstone around your neck. But before we deal with the nuts and bolts we must get you to think differently.

HE WON'T MEET ME IN MY BACK BEDROOM

A lot of people are very nervous of the back bedroom approach. In fact, a very pompous friend of mine, whose credit was so naff he couldn't even lease an office (though not through want of trying), was forced into his back bedroom, which he equipped as best he could to the limit of his credit line. When one day he decided he and I should collaborate on a project, he held his lapels, puffed out his chest, and donning his very best mid-Atlantic accent said, 'Hey Geoff, you're a crazy guy, but you've got talent and I want you on my team. Do you want to make the meet in your office or mine?' My wife, who is anything if not blunt, said 'Do you mean our back bedroom or yours?' He never spoke to us again. Sadly the ignominy of his situation drove him to find someone stupid enough to extend him enough credit to obtain all the things he felt his status demanded. He went bust, he did a bunk, and ruined his, and his family's lives. Please don't let it happen to you.

Some other, more realistic, people say, quite fairly, 'Oh, but I don't have the self-discipline to work at home,' and my reply is 'Nor do I, and ain't it lovely?' After all, if you haven't got some huge financial burden weighing you down, you don't have to be that disciplined. If you have done a good bit of work sitting on a dining chair at the old card table while doing the filing in a shoe box, you deserve to toddle off to the kitchen for a nice cup of coffee and a doughnut; perhaps even a glance at the newspaper wouldn't go amiss. If this riddles you with guilt, be assured I bet you are still ten times more efficient than you were in your old job. If the telephone rings and a client asks whether you could write a report on the kumquat crop of Lithuania, you say, 'OK chief, that will cost you £500,' and it takes you half a day. Well, don't feel guilty if you have got the rest of the day off. You probably would have stretched that report to a month in your old job. You would have got all stressed and stomach ulcery about it – a month is a long time on the kumquat market – and the company probably missed a window of opportunity, kumquat profit-wise. As it is, your client is well impressed to get the report in 24 hours, and you can stay cool. But remember to put on that show:

don't deliver in half a day, do it in 24 hours with comments like, 'I had to burn the midnight oil on this one a bit, but I appreciate the fragility of the kumquat market.'

It is, of course, clear that in this case the client has no idea what circumstances you are working under, and it always amazes me that with the aid of a huge extension lead, the phone and I can be literally anywhere. When I am not doing my face-to-face stuff or writing books (this particular bit was written in Sorrento, while listening to the siren of the Capri ferry), I do most of my work on the phone, but I could be sunning myself in the garden, or having a soak in the bath. The client hires my brain, and it works best in the sunshine. Maybe all companies should let their employees move outside to sunbeds on nice days.

Actually, this is not as much of a joke as it seems. Say you did work better on a sunbed, or wearing a country and western cowboy outfit, or while soaking your feet in a salt spa, then shouldn't your company allow you to work where you are at your best? Of course they won't, for all sorts of reasons or, to quote my first boss, 'You are here to work, not to enjoy yourself,' and when I asked him why I couldn't do both, he became my first ex-boss. But now you are your own boss, you must have the good judgement to let yourself work where and when you are happiest and can do your best work, because it is only your best work that will make you a good living.

POINTS TO PONDER

1 Optimistic arithmetic is fatal.
2 A list of things that smile: crocodiles, sharks, estate agents and office-equipment salesmen.
3 If you don't know what you are signing, see someone who does. If you think you know what you are signing, still ask for a second opinion from an expert. Dr Faust didn't.
4 Use the magic salesman-destroying spell: 'I want to think it over'. A day makes all the difference.

5 Salesmen are trained to handle you by making you their friend, but remember: friend or not, people do business to make money. Are you rich enough yet for people to make money out of you? Then say 'No'.

6 Life is just a bowl of toenails.

7 Be very, very realistic, even pessimistic, about your chances and you will still be amazed at how bad things can get.

8 Don't re-create your old working environment. The last thing you will need is a hat stand.

9 Develop the virtual office, the virtual car, and virtually anything else you need.

10 Don't let your clients know you are enjoying yourself. It might make them jealous.

5

The Money Spinners

There is a great deal of snobbery about the nouveaux riches. Whilst I violently disagree with that sort of envy-based criticism, I must say that when I have been around areas where the wealthy gather, there is often a quite definite broadening of accents. In the cast of our nouveaux riches friends, there seem to be some very rough types indeed, and certainly more than you would find in a normal cross-section of society. So why do so many of them make their million and how can we learn from it?

There must be something. The first and most obvious thing is that they started out by working very hard, but then that is something many of us are prepared to do. It is with great sadness that I see the couple at the Jolly Bunion Tea Shop working 24 hours a day, seven days a week for the six months that their fast-dwindling savings and ever-increasing overdraft will support their loss-making project. Hard work, therefore, is clearly not enough.

There is another key to the rough diamond's wealth-making. I would suggest that it is, ironically, their inability to borrow money. It is because of their roughness that the banks and even the leasing companies are very reluctant to lend them anything. When I ask these millionaires how they started, they tend to lean back against their Rolls Royces, light a large Havana cigar and give a little chuckle. The stories often sound like this: 'Well, of course, we were skint when we started and we only 'ad one, so when I heard this bloke wanted a thousand, Charley had to keep driving the same one round the block to make it look like we 'ad hundreds. Then when the bloke ordered, I 'ad to skin 'im for a 50-per-cent deposit 'cause I 'adn't got any money for materials. It was touch and go but he paid it and we worked night and day making the ruddy things in me mum's garden till the council threatened to evict her 'cause we were using welders. I remember the first load we sent out. We 'adn't got anyone to pack and load them, so we got all the lads out of the pub and I paid them with a barrel of beer that I got on tick. When the load was delivered, I was straight round the bloke's place for the cash.'

THE RECIPE FOR SUCCESS

If you translate that story carefully you find an almost perfect recipe for business success. Our hero, because of his low status with the bank, has not had the finance to create too much stock. He has been forced to use his powers of persuasion to sell on trust, and to get cash up front. There has been a casual no-cost occupation of premises, and the workforce has been employed on the most casual of casual basis. Finally and perhaps most importantly, the money for the job has been secured very quickly.

There is a little bit of a paradox here. While I counsel you most strongly not to attempt to re-create your old working environment, there are people out there, namely your potential clients, who are trapped by the constraints of tradition and may well expect certain 'standards'. If you are going into manufacturing or servicing you may have to have equipment, but the office furniture, fancy tills and so on are fripperies. If you haven't decided what sort of employment to give yourself, the cost of the equipment may be a deciding feature. Take one of my favourites which is window cleaning. The major cost is a bucket and you are in business. Actually that's a little unfair because you need a ladder, squeegees and leathers, but I am sure you get my point. In fact, with high-level business consultancy, you don't even need the bucket. But what if your client does expect the bells and whistles? Firstly you must be very honest with yourself, and decide why you want these things.

IT DOESN'T ADD UP

Say you have just lost your job, you are worried sick about the mortgage and so on, then a glimmer of light is offered in the shape of the idea of being self-employed. People give you encouragement, you go on a course, you begin to believe that opportunity beckons and you go out and get a brand-new car. Don't, please don't. Why did you do it? The reply is, 'Well I expect to do thousands of miles and the clients expect to see a decent vehicle.'

I once calculated for a large client the cost of a sales visit, and it went something like this. A car costs £15,000 and will lose at least £5,000 from its value in the first year. Finance costs £3,000. Insurance, servicing and tax is at least £2,000. Petrol works out at about 10p a mile. All things considered, if you do 10,000 miles in the first year, it will cost you £1.10 a mile. It would be cheaper to travel everywhere by hired, chauffeur-driven limousine.

If all you wanted out of life was a new car, then work to pay for it, but don't try to con yourself that it 'will pay for itself' or 'the taxman pays for it'. These are old wives' tales. Particularly the taxman thing. Sure if you make embarrassingly huge profits there are tax-efficient ways of getting yourself about in luxury, but those tax allowances come out of profit and in your first year or so, with all your setting up costs (even for a bucket), a profit is unlikely. 'The taxman pays for it' is even more stupid when you consider that it is your money we are talking about.

HAPPY TO PAY TAX

I have a very strange friend who is a highly successful market trader but is also scrupulously honest. Despite his honesty he loves to deal strictly in cash. One especially successful year, he made a clear, no-holds-barred £350,000. He told the tax office what he had made and, to their astonishment, they found he had been completely straight. He arrived to discuss this affair with £350,000 in a briefcase and they told him that the liability was £140,000. Without hesitation he paid up in bundles of tenners.

He describes it as one of the happiest days of his life. Don't be surprised. He walked from that office with nothing to hide, no fancy tricks and £210,000 that was all his. No more to pay. Nothing to write down. His to spend with an easy conscience. If and when you achieve the pleasure of having a case full of tax-paid money, you will find that you aren't in so much of a hurry to spend it.

A HIRE IMAGE

I suppose my business is established but I am in no hurry to spend my hard-earned money on a car or whatever. If you still insist that it isn't vanity, and you really do need a smart car for your business, try this.

Maybe you need to visit clients 100 miles away. Then go to your nearest main dealer and hire a brand spanking new car. Remember to horse trade a bit as we are currently paying £30 per day for a mid-range saloon. That works out at 15p per mile for the car, all insured, serviced and taxed, and 10p for fuel. That is 25p per mile, which is better than £1.10. More to the point, it cuts back on two more expenditures because if someone suggests that you pop here or there you tend to save up all your 'pops' to make it worth a day out. That saves you some cash, but much more importantly, saves you time. The truth is, I can't see how the hire companies can do it for the money, but then that isn't our problem.

Another tip here is that if you charge your clients a very modest 40p per mile for travelling expenses, you actually make a profit. When I started doing this, I calculated in my blackcurrant mode that two hirings a week would cost £3,000 a year (excluding fuel), which is considerably less than the depreciation on a mid-range saloon. Even if you totally destroy or lose the car, on the payment of a very reasonable deposit (about £50) the hire company will give you a new one with no blot on your record. If it busts, then leave it at the roadside for them to sort out, and pick up a fresh one. It is even 100-per-cent tax deductible because it is a straight hire with no private mileage.

So why the blackcurrant picking crack? The truth is I came nowhere near to two essential journeys a week. It averaged out at about one to one-and-a-half. In other words, I had absolutely no justification for owning a new car. If you try this you will find that the prospect of pay-as-you-drive actually makes you very economical, whereas if you owned the thing, you would feel the need to drive it lots just to justify it. For instance, if motoring costs you £10,000 a year, and you do 10,000 miles, that is a pound a mile, but if you do 100,000 miles it is 10p a mile. That is the sort of stupid mathematics that buries small enterprises.

This is just one example. You will find that all manner of goods and services can be hired, borrowed or scrounged. Sometimes it may seem expensive to 'hire', such as when the local shop charges you 10p a copy for photocopies and your own machine would be 2p. Over a year, however, even 1,000 copies would set you back only £100, which is much less than the cost of the service agreements on most machines, let alone the cost of ownership. If you do need huge numbers of copies, there are companies that lurk in industrial estates called reprographic houses that have copiers the size of small family bungalows and do monster runs in seconds at frighteningly low prices.

IF YOU'VE GOT IT, STASH IT

With a parsimonious attitude to your finances and a steady hand on the tiller, your next milestone will come when you realize that you have got the enterprise off the ground. Now it is making money, you could go out and buy all the kit you denied yourself at the beginning. The joke is that now you can afford it, you won't want it. Dare I make the suggestion that this is because the desire to re-create your old work environment and to continue the status that the company car brought was just a security blanket? The last vestiges of you as sales manager, as personnel manager, as head of research are gone, and now you are you, and have tasted the real unassailable status of doing your own thing. There is no need for flags or badges to say who you are.

Although I believe wholeheartedly in the idea that self-employment is the safest employment, I also accept that you can never be entirely sure of how much money you will make from month to month. You have a wave-shaped graph of income which illustrates good and bad times. How do you manage this, particularly if you have grown accustomed to a regular salary amount at the end of each month? Successful self-employed people make sure that their outgoings – business and personal – are never more than the profits of the worst possible trading year. Their mortgage is likely to be modest. Household goods are bought infrequently, and then with money saved or on interest-free credit, if there is any going. The loading, therefore, is very light, and I don't just mean financially. It is also light emotionally.

YOU CAN TELL A REAL MAN BY THE SIZE OF HIS MORTGAGE

When I first got married, I was terrified to discover that parents, friends and various in-laws measured the success of their nearest and dearest by the size of their mortgage. 'My Brian's doing well. He's just taken out a £75,000 mortgage.' Lenders calculate how much they will lend you on the size of your income, so I suppose that a larger mortgage tends to suggest a higher income.

Do you really need the 'five-bedroomed en-suite executive residence nestling in a dell of homes constructed lovingly with the young executive in mind'? Do you want to sign 25 years of your life blood away for that? Are you sure that once self-employment has given you back your own personality and the status that comes from self-reliance, you will feel the need to prove anything? A more modest home that you own outright frees your cash, frees your mind, and may save your soul.

There was a psychologist, I think it was Eric Berne, who suggested that for the working person in Western culture, a mortgage had become almost a genetic drive. He asserted that we are so conditioned to believe in the status of a mortgage – a burden we take up after the wild oats and fun of youth are over – that we carry it with pride to our grave, or at least until our useful working life is over. And if we haven't got one, we invent one. He argued that drug addiction, alcoholism or any other self-destructive habit are good substitutes for a mortgage as they have the same effect: creating a burden that is even harder to bear until it crushes the life out of you. Oh wizard!

Some people believe that losing their job was the worst possible thing that could have happened to them. If that job meant being proud of life-crushing burdens, losing it could be the very BEST thing that ever happened. The chance for a life without burden. When I was a hippy, one of my favourite Zen sayings was 'What a caterpillar calls death, we call a butterfly'. It is just that at the moment you are going through that chrysalis state and things might look a bit tough, but when you have spread those wings and felt that freedom, you will never want to be a caterpillar again. Just remember, though, things don't fly too well if they are overloaded.

TO DO WHAT'S EXPECTED OF US

Now we have done the hippy bit, we have to consider that paradox of what the customer expects. I remember once arriving in a hired car at a corporate client's offices, and the car I had happened to be in appeared to be the same as the client's. 'Oh, you have got a Smurwalt 200,' he observed. 'Is it the GL, GLS or GLSI?' 'I don't know,' I replied, and to my astonishment he went out to check. To his considerable satisfaction he discovered it to be the GLS which was the same as the one he had been issued with. This meant that we were of equal status and business could commence. If it had been the GL, I would have been his inferior, and if the GLSI, I would be superior. The company that he worked for had promoted this car-model pecking order, and something as small as a sunroof or CD player could make all the difference.

A company of my acquaintance tried giving a budget to their salesforce, and it wasn't long before some clever dick noticed that under certain circumstances a small Mercedes was cheaper to run than a Ford. When the Chairman saw his salespeople in shiny new Mercs, it didn't matter that they saved him money and impressed the clients. He fell into a carpet-chewing frenzy and the scheme was stopped forthwith.

THE WOBBLY CAR

My family owns one of those strange, very New-Age hippy Citroen 2CVs that are nicknamed 'flying dustbins' or 'tin snails'. They have a modest top speed, but they do have a removable roof so on sunny days you can putter along and soak up the rays. I used to toddle off to clients in this if I couldn't be bothered to hire and the kids didn't need it.

At this time, the government was giving grants to marketing companies to help small businesses, and one approached me. They offered to do a research project on my market. A no-cost offer like that would have been churlish to refuse. One of the things they particularly noticed was the car. 'A number of clients have picked up on that car of yours and they don't like it.' 'A bit down-market, you mean?' I asked. 'No, very much worse than that,' they replied, 'they think you are taking the piss.' Apparently, one client was rushing up the motorway in a large BMW to a life-or-death meeting. He overtook me in my 2CV, and he said that as I lolled there in the old Raybans, it looked as though I didn't have a care in the world – and he wanted to stop and kill me. He felt that the car, like all cars, made a statement, and that the statement in this case was a single digit raised vertically to the world.

The whole philosophy of this book should transport you to a parallel universe where life is happier, but as you need to work with your old world, it might be a good idea not to look too alien. The real problems commence, however, when you choose an enterprise that constantly interfaces with the other side, because the public will judge you on the quality of your presentation.

To fly in the face of all I have said previously, I do tend to judge quality on the presentation in the case of professional services, restaurants and so on. It is alright to have a back-bedroom operation as long as the client doesn't know. You could prepare a meal on a camping gas stove in your coal shed, but to get good money for it you must serve it on starched linen adorned with heavy silver cutlery. This isn't really a contradiction so much as a realignment of priorities. Where our earlier friends were spending money on limed-oak desks and thick upholstered swivel chairs, I would spend the money on the area where my clients got their impression of my operation. This, of course, may influence your choice of business because if you have chosen, say, a restaurant, it has to be good. Bits of dayglo paper in the window with 'Today's Special' written on them in felt pen tend to create a certain price expectation from the customer, and not a very high one, I can assure you.

In my last book, *Resistance is Useless*, which is mostly about selling and persuasion, I tried to illustrate the story of a man who needs life-saving surgery, and because of the waiting list on the National Health Service, decides to go private. He is quoted £15,000 and is so shocked by this price that he drops into his local pub to drown his sorrows. He is telling his friend about this when a strange little man sidles up to him and explains that he is Cyril Boggis of the 'Reading Amateur Surgery Club'. 'We meet up the Nag's Head on a Tuesday. I'm a VAT inspector by trade, but I do a bit of bowel resectioning in my spare time. I would love to have a poke around inside you. No charge, I do it for fun. We'll even have a little bit of quiche after, if you survive.' Would you let him touch you? It is obvious that professionalism is vital to financial success, but professionalism is only an im-pression and one we can create.

YOU ONLY CRY ONCE WHEN YOU BUY QUALITY

It always amazes me that start-up businesses tend to buy the new car, the computer, the electronic till and so on, and yet the impression they make is very unprofessional. I find the reasons for this quite hard to understand, but we ought to try, so this is my stab at it. I suppose it must be perceived value from the old dimension to the new. A thousand pounds for a computer gives you one nice big plastic box with what is tantamount to a colour television on top, and loads of gubbins inside. On the other hand, paying £500 for a bit of design work gets you maybe four or five bits of tracing paper with squiggles on. That is half the price of a computer for a few tatty bits of paper, but the fact is that, if chosen well, those tatty bits of paper can pay you back a million-fold.

A distant and very elderly relative of mine was a designer long before the war. He was once approached by a firm of Greek origin. Their name escapes me, but it was something like Papangypolinyos. They made, before these health-conscious days, a rather fine Virginia cigarette, but the consumer was having trouble asking for '20 Papangypolinyos'. The company asked my relative whether he could help. They got a handful of scrappy tracing paper that said quite simply 'John Player', and had the picture of a sailor.

A Mr Bird approached him about a simple name for his custard company. He drew a huge yellow chicken. 'What's a huge yellow chicken got to do with custard?' asked the client. Both of these brands have become classics. Of course, they were excellent products supported by super designs.

BEANS OR WAREHOUSES

As a result of a surprise bequest, you find you have a choice of two legacies. The first is a factory worth five million, and the other is just a name which you can use as your own. The name happens to be Heinz. Well, I know for certain which I would take and it ain't the bricks and mortar. Your image, your impact, the thing that people recognize you for, is therefore worth investing in.

You and your partner go to that new restaurant in town, and the menu is a typed sheet in a standard perspex menu holder. The quality and taste of the food are unlikely to make up for that clanger. See what people do even in value-for-money places. There is a big difference between Pizza Hut, McDonalds and the Greasy Spoon transport caff, even though the pricing structure is similar.

Where I live there is a burger bar which I always thought was part of a major franchise chain. It is a little dearer than the Burger Kings and the McDonalds, but then the burgers are that much better. The only strange thing is that in other towns where I was sure they would be, I could never find one. As they are quite clearly the best, I asked my local manager where the other branches were. He grinned, 'There's only one other, and I own that too.'

WHAT PIRACY TAUGHT ME

The manager has achieved a marketing classic. It is called benchmarking. In other words, he has used his competitors as a benchmark, or given them a score on a number of different areas which he needs to exceed to take them on. It seems so obvious, but people cheerfully ignore the implications.

When I was a kid, we used to play board games, and one of my favourites was called 'Buccaneer', a pirate game, with little ships, a map of Treasure Island and real bits of treasure. You had a crew with certain powers of fighting, sailing and what not. When you were laden with treasure, you set off for your home port but you could be waylaid by your opponent. If his crew's skill outnumbered yours, you would lose the treasure to him, have your crew wiped out, and suffer the ignominy of getting blown to Mud Bay. The point is that only a fool would set off with what he knew to be a weak crew because defeat would then be inevitable.

If, for instance, you wanted to open a hotel, you would benchmark, say, Trust House Forte. Don't panic for a moment. Just do it and then we can analyse the results. We must look at the staff: their attitude, training, pay, level of skill and their uniforms. What about the accommodation? How does it look? Is there an en-suite bathroom? What sort of soaps are supplied? Is there a television in the room and, if so, does it provide satellite channels? Then on to the restaurant. What sort of menu does it offer, how well is the food presented ... well, you get the idea, don't you?

To start with, whatever your type of business, take your most prestigious competitor and do this exercise. I know we want to be a guerrilla and to travel light, but that is no excuse to be crap. A freedom fighter who under- or overestimates his super-power enemy, is a dead freedom fighter. It doesn't mean you can't take them on and win, but you must be fit to win. You must deserve to win because you are qualified to do so.

Imagine staying at a private house which is also a hotel, and finding little boxes of genuine 'Dun Roaming' soap, a satellite television in your room, no crinoline doll covering the bog roll, and a choice of modern stylish food for dinner, or freshly squeezed orange juice for breakfast. If you take the big boys on at their own game, and then add personal service, you can charge more, not less. There is a Regency terrace B&B in Torquay that charges £12.50 per night; a night in a Trust House Forte hotel will cost you around £65; and there is a Regency terrace house in London that charges £240 per night. Why? Answer that and you could be charging £240 instead of £12.50. It is just a recipe. Break it down into its ingredients and do exactly the same. That is benchmarking.

Even those of you who are tempted into a one-person, on-your-toes type enterprise (which I favour) will benefit from good presentation. Consultancy is one area where disaster awaits the unprepared. People apply a kind of bizarre logic. I meet with them and they hand me some truly dreadful stock-printed (or even hand-printed) business card, and even worse, when I ask them for any literature, I get something truly naff that has come off the desk-top publishing function of their computer. Listen, if you are trying to be a svelte international business consultant, you are doomed if you present people with a horrid clip art image of a cartoon shouting into a megaphone with the words 'You have tried the rest, now try the best' coming out of the end. These people tell me that they have researched their market and discovered that the big consultancy outfits are charging £1,000 per consultant day. They go on to tell me that they would be happy with £1,000 a week, therefore they could take the job on for a fifth of the competition.

The point is, however, that the client expects the consultant to give advice that could change every aspect of his company, put people out of work, into work. It could involve massive investment. It is the amateur surgeon thing again. No one in their right mind hires cut-price consultants. Where does that leave you – up against the monster competitor? If you are capable of turning things upside down, it can leave you in a very strong position indeed. The big competitor may have plenty of skilled practitioners but they are faceless and infinitely interchangeable. But with you, there is only you, and if it is only you the customer wants, they will have to pay at a premium, not a discount.

Look, the Tom Peterses, the Sir John Harvey-Joneses, the Charles Handys, the Geoff Burches, the Raymond Blancs, the Lord Lichfields, the Nicos, they could all be described in pejorative terms as one-man bands, but all of them place a premium value on being unique. All we have to do is make you a marketable and highly desirable item which we will do in the marketing bit. Rest assured – your presentation in the shape of the impression you make is what fixes the price in your customers' minds. In areas of business where the customers come to you in quantity, such as restaurants and so on, this can be a very expensive process, but even here, there are wrinkles you can use. Take the bistro approach, which means you can use old church pews, have a calligrapher handwrite your menus on velum, and a quality atmosphere can be generated at a relatively modest cost, but one sniff of a red paper napkin or a polythene tomato ketchup bottle, and you are dead in the water.

IT'S ALL IN THE NAME

The twee-name syndrome is another area that makes me wince. I know you're excited as in your mind you make that definite commitment to do your own thing. The germ of an idea has grown to a happy pustule of great plans and schemes, as you sit snuggled up with your partner in front of a crackling log fire, and plan your next move. Then fate decrees that before all else, before you have ascertained where you will make a living, or whether you could stand smiling at awful people for the next 20 years, before all these things, you decide to choose a clever name.

It is one of those truly odd things that we personally would-n't do business with a company that had a twee name, yet we have this lemming-like compulsion to pick one for ourselves. Perhaps it is a lack of personal confidence that makes us christen our enterprise with a wall of naffness that we can hide behind. I think you ought to know that I have a deep need for everyone to love me, and because of this I have picked examples that should be wild enough to miss specific targets and to avoid offending you, but in the case of twee names it seems there is no excess that you won't go to, so I am sure to brass someone off.

There are the cliché classics: the Corkers wine bars, the Mad Hatters tea shops, the Cut Above hair salons. Nothing wrong with these, of course, except that they have been done before. Then there is the ultra-clever and original that makes you laugh, like a firm that sells hat stands mail-order, and decides to call itself 'Stand and Deliver'.

Before you stop chuckling in glee at your clever idea and set it in concrete, take a walk down the high street and look at the most successful names: Dixons, Woolworths, Boots, WH Smith, Sears, Ford, Wendy's and, of course, Marks and Spencer. If we had our way, it should be Nix 'n' Bras. The main objection I have to even the least cringe-making name is that it sets in stone for-ever the original idea that you set off with. That is every aspect of the time the business was started, the work that it did, the geographical area, and the quality of the target market. If you started a clothes shop in the Midlands in the 1960s and called it 'Fab Gear of Brum', you would be right up the creek now.

I CONFESS

To prove I am not picking on you, I will admit that my major qualification for being so critical about twee names is that I did it myself. About a million years ago when I started my consultancy, sales training was in vogue, and that is what I started up doing. Falling immediately into the twee-name trap, I tried to find a cleverdick name that would sum up what I did. A trainer, that's what I was, so what could be a more zesty, punchy, up-to-the-minute name for a trainer? What better than a coach? With that, 'Sales Coach' was born. If you are feeling kind, you might think that this isn't a bad name for a sales training outfit. Bad or not, I became a hostage to it, and it wasn't long before my talent and my business set off in interesting but unpredictable directions, and 'Sales Coach' became an anachronism, as I am not really a sales trainer anymore.

Why did I choose a name? Why does anybody? Maybe it is something to hide our lack of professionalism behind or, much more to the point, a symptom of a lack of confidence. The major target of this book is for lone individuals to employ themselves, and make a reasonable to substantial living. A good reputation adds value. This could even be expressed as fame. Famous people get lots of money because their name tells you there is only one of them, and the fame tells you that they are in demand. When we think of fame we bring to mind television, the national press, and so on, but you can be a famous window cleaner in 20 streets. If they all know how good you are and that there is only one of you, that adds value.

If you consider Raymond Blanc, David Bailey, Jasper Conran or his dad, I suppose you could call them tradespeople, but they have traded under their names and have given that name enormous value. If you use your own name, building its value isn't the only advantage. It also gives much more flexibility. If the enterprise is called 'Pipeline Advice', the owner would argue that their name helps potential customers spot what they do. I would use the same argument against it in as much as that is what the business will be stuck doing, whereas if it was called 'David Higgins Design' with, if you must, Pipeline Advice in brackets underneath, you can take up other opportunities.

NEVER TOO PROUD TO DECORATE

I have a very dear friend who gives marketing advice (and very good he is at it too), but the other day I saw him up a ladder decorating the outside of someone's house. His explanation was that he had a couple of days off and heard that the house owner was offering around £1,000 pounds for the decorating. In a flash he had shed his suit and was up the ladder. The invoice the customer got had the name at the top and was the same invoice the multinational would have got for advice on trans-Siberian export strategy.

As I came to understand and take advantage of this flexibility myself, the GEOFF BURCH bit of my cards and notepaper has expanded, and the Sales Coach bit has shrunk away to almost nothing. If you decorate wedding cakes and call the outfit 'Tiers before Bedtime' or some such name, you won't be able to offer to design the dress or do the catering as well, but if you had called yourself 'Mary Scrunge Events', you could be much more flexible.

THOUGHT OF FRANCHISING?

Make no mistake, some fly-by-night franchising deals are a horrible, terrifying rip-off that will skin you and hang you out to dry, but the established ones with good track records could save you a lot of heartache. The more popular burger outfits and printers are prime examples. You may be shocked at the cost of setting one up, but that is the real cost, and the tough but successful people who run these organizations are buying in for you at the best possible price. They have done their sums, they know the trade, and if you listen to them they can put you on the track to a good future.

Why are tough, ruthless people good for you in this instance? There is a rude but apposite saying that sums it up: 'It is better to have them in your tent pissing out than outside your tent pissing in'. Just be very careful that you choose an established player. Get your bank to check them out, and speak to loads and loads of other franchisees, and not just the ones they recommend. If you do choose this route, you move somewhat out of my remit, and there are many more detailed books on franchises.

MY MUM COULD, SO CAN YOU

Another way to short-circuit things a bit is to buy a going (or even ex-going) concern. My mum used to make ends meet or even overlap by buying rundown businesses, usually with living accommodation. I have lived behind wool shops, over supermarkets, and even in a converted cow shed at the back of a dairy. She would live off the profits and build the business to a peak, whereupon she would sell it for substantially more than she paid for it.

This exercise takes a great deal of bottle and hides many pitfalls. Why is the other person selling? Does their previous success mean they have played the market out, or the novelty of the operation has worn off? What if they have been losing money and want out? Are you sure you are so much cleverer and can turn it round? The problem is we are all convinced we can, and that we have spotted something or have found an angle that the other person hasn't, but for me the warning comes in my own home town. There are three sites in particular: one has tea shops that always go bust, one has wine bars that always go bust, and one has restaurants that always go bust. Same site, same type of enterprise, same outcome, but each time the new owner must believe they can pull it off.

Again, let me counsel you against positive thinking and remind you of the grizzly death that waits for optimists. Icy cool realism is what is needed here, and if you are really cold hearted, wait for your target business to go bust and vulture up all the bits and pieces at auction for a song. Just make sure it is not your bones that end up getting picked over.

In the case of my mum's success, she had found a simple common denominator. The businesses were quite well positioned, there were a good few potential customers, nothing fancy was being tried. What they all lacked was the owners' ability to sell. When mum applied her unparalleled talents as a salesperson, and added some ruthlessly shrewd buying (which is just the other side of the same coin), the businesses were transformed. Subsequent owners never quite matched her prodigious ability to build turnover. So, I prescribe for you a few sound selling skills, and that is where we are off to in the next chapter or so.

POINTS TO PONDER

1 Why should the nouveaux riches have all the best techniques?
2 They succeed because they can't borrow money.
3 If you really think you need something, beg, borrow, steal or even short-term hire, but wait before buying or leasing. It could cost you everything.
4 Travel light and stay alive. Even if you are making money, prepare to ride out feast and famine. Don't believe a big loan can represent big status.
5 Don't flaunt your freedom and high spirits to your clients. Create the sober front that they expect or they may feel you are ridiculing their standards. OK, you might be doing just that, but letting them know isn't good for business.
6 Money spent on quality image making gives a better return than money spent on useless hardware.
7 Benchmark or compare yourself to your competitors. If you don't beat them clearly in a number of areas (not price), you are doomed. Don't despair, just get better now.
8 One-person bands should be proud enough to charge more for their exclusivity.
9 Never pick a twee name. You will become a hostage to it and it will come back and haunt you.
10 Maybe you want to take on a franchise or established business. It can save you all the hassle of setting up, but be careful: if they couldn't make money, maybe you can't either.

6

Now Ask Someone to Buy Something

Later on in this bit of the book, we are going to get all clever and sophisticated. We will investigate the subtle ways and wiles you can use to entwine your customer in a web of buying experiences that will bring huge pleasures and rewards to both of you. For now, let's just consider the gritty basics.

Salespeople are always justifying their existence by chanting, mantra like, the clichés of their profession, such as 'Production minus sales equals scrap', or 'Nothing happens until someone sells something', or, my favourite, 'Finding and keeping customers is the only activity that generates income. All other activities generate cost'. However much you may dislike salespeople and their wicked ways, the unfortunate thing is that all of those sayings are irrefutably true, particularly the last one. Your scheme can literally stand or fall on the outcome of your ability to sell either your product or yourself, preferably both. If you are now worried that you don't have an ability to sell, you should be. Without it you are doomed, but then again, it is not as difficult as some would have you believe, and we will soon have you stuffing huge wads of tenners into the old back pocket.

I guess when I say salesperson, you have this picture in your mind of some oily thing that wears too much aftershave, has gold fillings and a propensity to leap out from behind a yucca plant and force you into buying a car you don't want. In actual fact, the very best salespeople are the ones you don't recognize. The ones that listen sympathetically to your problems without interrupting, the ones that gently help you to understand what it is you need, to put your world to rights. Through their encyclopaedic knowledge, they will find the best way to help you own these things. As we discovered in previous chapters, you don't want to be on the receiving end of that lot, but may I suggest you should seriously consider being on the transmitting end?

Where do we start? The beginning? No, lets annoy all my professional sales-training chums and start at the end.

PROSPECTING, OR THERE'S GOLD IN THEM THAR HILLS

As you may have noticed, I have tried so far to steer clear of jargon, but as we are encroaching on a professional discipline, you will have to pick up some of the buzz words in case you want to study further and then find you don't understand what the gurus are on about. In classic sales terms, the end of the sale is referred to as the 'close'. Up until this point, entertainingly enough, what we mortals would call a 'customer' isn't one yet. No. Apparently you officially become a customer when you have bought something. Until this point you are the 'prospect'. In other words, you are a prospective customer, and the tub-thumpers will, if allowed, start drivelling on about gold mines and prospecting.

Personally I find it quite dangerous to allow salespeople to see people not as customers, because when you say 'I'm just looking', the greasy-smile approach swiftly becomes the contemptuous wander off. Everybody out there is your customer, it's just that a few of them don't know it yet. Apparently, in some of the more esoteric sales manuals, the received wisdom suggests that when you have that preliminary interview with the 'prospect', you aren't trying to find out what they would like to buy. You are in fact 'qualifying' them or, to put it another way, you are determining whether or not they have the qualifications to allow them the honour of doing business with you. There is a sort of logic to this, albeit fairly twisted logic. You see, they maintain that there is little point talking to a 15-year-old with no money about buying a Rolls Royce. The reason they would give is that being too young to drive and being skint would 'dis-qualify' him from buying.

The problem I encounter with this when training sales-people is that it breeds an overbearing arrogance. It is an approach that suggests every salesperson is so wildly busy that every precious second can only be lovingly devoted to the serious cash-in-hand buyer. To avoid wasting these vital minutes, the God-like salesperson will qualify you within seconds of your entry into his helter-skelter life. If it is a car showroom and the eagle eye of the salesperson has detected a shortfall in the dress code he has laid down for a qualified prospect, you will be dismissed as what they call a 'tyre kicker', and ignored. What if the 15-year-old kid's dad is a millionaire and values his childrens' opinion on what the family would enjoy as a car?

START THE BEGINNING AT THE END

Anyway, enough of this. Let's get back to starting at the end, if you see what I mean. The thing that intimidates the professional salesperson the most is the end. The point where they have to get a firm decision to buy. Everything in their eyes has been swimming along nicely, and in a funny sort of way, they have become your chum, but here is the catch-22: the easiest people to sell to are people who like you. People won't like you if you suddenly start asking them to buy things. The temptation, therefore, is to carry on being the customer's chum without ever asking them to buy anything.

This hiatus has, in consequence, become the focus of a great deal of philosophical discussion. The sales trainers and gurus treat it as the point of true enlightenment to the seekers of the sales-path way. They will tell you that if you can master the close, all success will come your way. There are many techniques of closing the sale which we might have a gander at when we get to the sophisticated bit, but for now we will look at the simplest and most neglected: to simply ask someone to buy something.

When was the last time someone came straight out with it and asked you to buy something? Maybe while reading this book you have already started your project. You have been to see a potential client, customer or even, if you like, prospect. It has all gone very well; you have come away feeling truly chipper, but wait just a moment. Did you actually ask them to buy? Why not? The answers I get to that question tend to be 'The time wasn't quite right', 'I think they were very interested and will be back in touch', 'Things were going so well I didn't want to cock things up by putting pressure on them to buy'.

VERY INTERESTED ISN'T

When I have got my sales-training hat on, we work with salespeople to try and improve their game. Obviously they visit or see many customers who don't necessarily buy on the spot, and their sales managers, in an effort to find out what's going on, demand some kind of written report. When I am given a pile of these reports, I know what they will say before I even look. The classic line in the comments section is 'V. interested'. Sometimes there is a little bit of pointless preamble like 'No definite requirement at present, but v. interested'. 'Loves our price, but needs board approval. V. interested'. I go around with these people on a one-to-one basis. I talk to them after the event, and they present me with 'V. interested' or, when they are more sophisticated, 'V. int'. 'But,' I cry, 'You didn't once ask the customer to buy. Not even a gruff "Well do you want one or not?"' By the way, that last sentence will get every sales trainer spinning in their grave because it breaks just about every rule of selling, but I think even that can be justified against the current dismal failure rate.

What a refreshing change then to meet you lot, people without preconceived ideas, people who need success, people with genuine enthusiasm and belief. I have my potential millionaires gathered, and we look through some of the research you have been doing and the results of the meetings you have had with your future customers. Perhaps you have made a note of what went on, and how you thought it went. May I see? I can guess why you are a bit shy because you have written 'Very Interested', haven't you? The problem is that it is even more dangerous for you to write this than our worldly salesperson. At least he doesn't believe it anymore, but you might. You could be tempted to go home and add up all your 'V. ints' and think they represent real business. Just like my blackcurrants, 'V. ints' are illusory and should most certainly not be banked on.

Before we get on to any of the nuances and subtleties of closing or, for that matter, even opening sales, let's just get you over that initial hurdle of simply having the intention to sell and asking the customer to buy something.

THEY JUST DIDN'T SELL

I like to pride myself on my ability to spot enterprises that are doomed to failure. In some cases, as in the 'Rent a Rodent' story in Chapter 2, it is pretty obvious. But I also feel that I can spot the more hopeful ones.

In one of my groups recently there was a woman who had quite a good idea for a cake-icing business. It's not a new idea, and that strongly counted in her favour, as established, well-tried ventures have a much better chance than new ideas. But more than that, she had real talent. She had brought samples, and her ability to make aeroplanes, football team shields and wedding cakes was unsurpassed. The cakes inside were distinctly yummy as well, which was a very major plus point. The whole project looked good and it passed all my mental checks: she didn't expect a high income; it was a cash business; she already had all the equipment she needed; and it worked very well out of her existing domestic kitchen. Imagine my surprise when I saw our erstwhile entrepreneur working at the checkout in my local supermarket.

'What are you doing here?' I asked.
'Oh, things weren't going that well so I got a proper job,' she replied. 'I spent all that money on moulds and things,

and hardly anybody bought anything.'
'You mean you didn't sell anything?'
'That's what I said.'

No, that's NOT what she said. She said 'No one bought'. I said she didn't sell. Did you know she was making fancy cakes? If she had asked you outright to buy one, would you have turned her down flat? It doesn't matter, because in the event she didn't give you the chance. Instead, she sat in her kitchen waiting for people to come and ask her to do them a cake. Take it from me, you don't get a lot of passing trade in the galley kitchen of a suburban semi. Sure, she put the odd cheap advertisement in the local free paper, and some cards in the newsagent's window, and yes, these brought in some work and a lot of enquiries that, through her lack of skill, she failed to convert into business.

This book may lean towards the cutting-edge, New-Age, caring, personal fulfilment-style of business, but there are also good old business chestnuts which are still 'v. useful'. One of them, which is particularly apposite here, is a cartoon, much loved of salespeople, which shows two vultures on a branch. One vulture is saying to the other, 'Patience my arse. I'm going to go out and kill something.' Think very carefully about this dubious witticism. It is telling you a solid truth. This enterprise is your future, and its success depends on your ability to get off your butt and physically promote it. Yes, better still SELL IT. MAKE IT HAPPEN. It is entirely in your power, or give up right now and sit at that checkout with a 'proper job'.

WHEN WAS THE LAST TIME SOMEONE SOLD YOU ANYTHING?

What should our cake-icer have done? To start with, she should have asked people to buy her cake. Sure, we are going to deal with the sale steps, the clever cut and thrust of selling skills, but firstly you must be sure that you are asking people to buy things. When we talk about selling, the uninitiated start to go on about high-pressure selling, not taking no for an answer, and forcing people to buy things they don't want. I am sure you will, if asked, cite a number of examples of salespeople who get up your nose by their intrusive ways, but just think for a moment: when was the last time that someone actually came right out and asked you to buy?

OK, I know you may have been in the local hi-fi store and had some oily nerd creep up behind you and say, 'Aren't those magnificent? Is that the kind of equipment you wanted?', or, worse, 'Can I help you?' while gently rubbing their hands in a kind of washing-the-blood-off way. You reply, 'No thanks, just looking' and scuttle off. We analyse approaches and whatnot later, but the point I make quite basically is: were you asked to buy anything?

'Well, do you want that? Shall I wrap it for you?' A little brutal and unsophisticated, I grant you, but a good starting point for us and our cake-icer. If you look at her potential market (which is the whole world), you will understand the opportunity she is missing. Take a look into the street: everyone walking past knows somebody who might want a fancy cake. Perhaps a child who is about to celebrate a birthday, someone who is getting married, or someone who is soon to have their baby christened. Does she, or you, have the brass neck to leap out at strangers and say 'Hi, nice to meet you,' (tiny bit of jolly chitchat here to pad things out). 'Tell me, do you know any kids? Your nephew – going to be six next birthday? When is that? Seven weeks, not long – bit of a little terror is he? Imagine his face if he had a cake shaped like a shark with glowing red eyes! He's what? Blood-thirsty? Well, in that case, we could put a diver in its jaws with a bit of red icing blood. No, they're not expensive, they just take a little time to make, but if you give me a deposit today you can be sure of a wonderful surprise for his birthday.'

BETTER A NAFF APPROACH THAN NO APPROACH AT ALL

You may consider this a fairly naff and unsubtle approach, and I may even accept that you are right, but it is better than no approach at all. If it provokes a 'get stuffed' from nine out of ten people, and only gets one yes, that would have still insured our cake-icer's success.

One of the things that annoys me about the high-pressure, foot-in-the-door insurance/double glazing/vacuum salespeople, is their cliché that the selling process is a numbers game. For instance, if 3 out of 100 buy then see 500 to make 15 sales. If you want to double sales, then see 1,000. It annoys me because I feel that their efforts could be far more focused and targeted. The reason the other 97 don't buy is because of the sales technique and not dislike of the product. So, to contradict myself completely, the numbers game is the best place to begin.

BE BORING. IT'S BORING THAT GETS TO THE OIL

Be prepared to become a bore. I know this may be a horrifying prospect for you, but remember that your life (well your livelihood at least) depends on it. We are so poor at self-promotion, but it is the key to getting a flying start.

Our American cousins don't seem to have our reticence. You only have to whisper to a friend in a restaurant that you may need a little repair work, and about 750 million people leap on you with business cards: 'Hey buddy, sorry to interrupt your meal right there, but I couldn't help overhearing your conversation, and I thought I ought to introduce myself. My name is J.B.J. Sheckenberger the 15th and I run just about the finest repair shop this side of the Mississippi. Take my card right here, and I'll personally make sure you get a real great deal.'

Before you start on about being brash or intrusive, bear in mind that this fellow's big open smile and genuine enthusiasm wins most people over. We have a completely misguided idea that it is somehow inappropriate to promote our enterprise at every opportunity. What were you before becoming your own boss? Design engineer? Personnel manager? Whatever you did, you were probably spoiled as regards the way your work came to you. You finished one bit, be it a design or a consultation, and another bit would be put in front of you. Didn't you wonder where this work came from? Perhaps you peeked out from your 10th-story office window to see 'Mister too sharp for his own good', the company sales representative, oiling off somewhere in his lovely shiny car that was paid for by your honest sweat. What do people like that do all day, save swan around the country's motorways, stopping only to quaff vast quantities of fine food and drink on expenses, and to knock a round of golf with people of a similar persuasion? I suppose it isn't vaguely possible that this contemptible person may in some way be connected to the work that we get given to do.

Although I have trained salespeople, I also find it difficult to make the connection between the sales process and the work the company does. Salespeople themselves have an equally frightening habit of reversing this process in as much as they forget that the promises they make to secure their sales commission have to be kept by somebody back at base. When the connection is made, however, the results are quite unusual.

THE CASE OF THE CHEERING WELLY BOOT

For some bizarre reason, I was visiting a welly boot factory in the USA, and I was being shown the main production area. This was a thundering place of noises and smells where sweating workers on clattering presses hammered off the vital components of the wellies. Imagine my surprise when a man in a smart suit walked down through the factory, and as he did the machines shut down one by one. The operators started whooping and cheering in a way that only Americans can. 'Hey guys, here's Frank.' 'Whoop, whoop,' 'Lets hear it for Frank,' 'Whoop Yo,' 'High five Frank, yo whoop.' This apparition gave them a clenched-fist salute, which provoked a roar of approval, and he disappeared through a door, at which point everyone returned to work. I asked my guide:

'Who was that?'
'That was Frank,' he beamed.
'I think I gathered that, but why all the fuss?'

'Well, Frank is our northwestern sales guy, and he has just secured the biggest order for boots we have ever had, so all the guys in the plant are saying a great big thank you for their jobs.'

As luck would have it, almost as soon as I returned home, I had cause to visit a welly boot factory over here. It was the same as the American version in almost every detail, and over the roar of the machines I recounted the 'Frank' story. The manager who was showing me round looked at me with the sort of sympathetic smile that one usually reserves for the saddest of deluded loonies. 'Tell you what, lad. If any one of the salespeople set foot in this factory, the lads would be bouncing the wellies off his head – bringing us all this extra work, pillock.'

I suppose it is a cultural thing but whatever it is, you are now production, marketing, accounts and SALES, and without abilities in these areas you are in deep trouble, especially when it comes to sales. The biggest asset you could start with is a full order book, so no matter how nervous it makes you or how much you feel that it is 'not quite nice' to promote yourself, lose no opportunity to do so. As you stand on the deck of the sinking ship while panic reigns all around you, smile gently at your fellow passengers and engage them in conversation. 'Golly, bit of a do all this. I hope we don't all drown. You know they would have all been safer with the all-new Floatamat pocket life jacket that I manufacture. Look, here's my card. Give me a ring if you survive this.' Or, if you see a decorator plunge off a ladder and a crowd gathering, be prepared to fight your way through while waving your card above your head and chirping, 'Let me through, I provide accident insurance.' OK, maybe a bit over the top, but get the point and lose no opportunity to promote and introduce yourself. Better still, create opportunities to do it. If you sell booze, get invited to parties; if you are an accountant, get involved in business clubs and don't be reticent about pedalling your cards around. Even if you become a bit of a bore, at least you will be a happy, well-fed and solvent bore, which for now is good enough.

THE FROTH ON THE COFFEE

Obviously I am interested in taking my art to the very highest levels, and I study the latest sales technique and nuances with an appetite, but it never ceases to amaze me how the simplest approach often works.

Let's imagine that you have put your all into this tea shop or coffee bar. What now? Shall we hope for some business? I trust you picked a good position because tea shops and coffee bars need the passing trade. You stand or fall, then, on the whims of the capricious customer. Not if you were born in Sorrento, you don't. While I was there writing some of this book, I sat in a pavement café and watched the waiters. They leapt out on passing shoppers and tourists, 'Hello good friend, stop and have a lovely cappuccino with me. Sit here, the best seat, and I'll bring you the menu.'

I know what you are thinking – that somehow it is intrusive and may put people off – but they were succeeding with at least one in ten, and their café was packed out. Anyway, with their humour and lovely open smiley faces, they didn't put anyone off, and when you did sit down, they put on a show which kept the customers constantly delighted and hankering to return to repeat the experience. We'll look at this technique in more detail soon, but for now, accept that bringing in business, however difficult it may be for you, is entirely in your hands.

Don't come back in a few months time with a dreary tale that the work 'just didn't come in', because I have one of those jester's pig's bladders on a stick, and to add to the ignominy of you losing your shirt on your business enterprise, I shall whop you round the earhole with it. You want a secure future? Then make it happen.

RULE ONE: ASK PEOPLE TO BUY SOMETHING

I walk into your greengrocer's shop and say, 'Excuse me, how much are your cauliflowers?' 'They're 67p, sir' you reply, quick as a flash. 'OK, then I'll have one.' What was the last thing you sold? Before you reply 'a cauliflower', remember that waiting pig's bladder, because the truth is you sold me nothing.

There is a modest-sized greengrocer near me that, under normal circumstances, shouldn't be making a decent living, but when I saw the dear old gentleman who runs it swanning around town in his Bentley, I felt it was time to investigate. I suggest that you walk in there to buy a cauliflower. His beaming smile will greet you.

'Good morning to you, what can I do for you?'

'Those cauliflowers.'

'Oh, yes m'dear,' (I live in Gloucestershire) 'Lovely firm-'earted beauties. Tell me, are you going to eat it tonight my luv? I tell you why I asked: I've just had the first crop of the Canaries new potatoes in, little waxy beauties, peels themselves they do, 'ad some for me own tea last night. They'd go a treat with that cauli. Let's pop in a couple of pounds of them. By the way, how are your kiddies in this cold snap? Tell you a funny story, I was driving along in the van with Charlie, an' I heard this huge gurt BANG! "What's that?" I says, and Charlie says, "That's them oranges boss, they're exploding with vitamin C" – half a dozen of them will keep your kids fit and healthy.'

'How much is that?'

'Well, yer cauli, 67p, the spuds 90p, the oranges 44p, that be two pound and a penny, let's call it two pound for cash, thanking you. By the way, I've got my Christmas satsumas in next week, and I knows how you love the juicy little darlings, so I'll put some aside for you, but don't call in before Thursday so you can be sure I'll have 'em ready for you.'

Let's just consider for a moment what he has done. The first thing he succeeded in doing was at least tripling his turnover. Stop for a moment and think about that. It would mean that if you bought a little run-down shop that turned over £50,000 a year and just about broke even, you could, if you had this bloke's talent, boost that to £150,000 just by your ability to sell. I am not suggesting it is a skill that might be worth acquiring, but one that is positively essential to your survival.

If our little grocer had ever taken the time to read one of those super high-powered American sales manuals, he would see he had just about completed the perfect, text-book sale by making sure that not only was the customer given the opportunity to buy the maximum at the time, but was also invited back, thereby ensuring future business from that customer. It was a virtuoso performance, and he never read a sales book in his life, but then he is a natural and you may not be, and that is why you are reading this. Don't despair, however, because with a few simple tools, we can make even the greengrocer envious. Remember rule one: ASK PEOPLE TO BUY SOMETHING.

You stand at the counter of your continental coffee bar, and two ladies order a coffee each. What have you just sold them? Careful, remember the pig's bladder, that's right, nothing. So, now's your chance. Assuming that you do what I always do and start without reading all the instructions, I will accept that you haven't acquired the dazzling and sophisticated skill that the rest of this book will provide you with. What your current skill can arm you with is the knowledge that if you ask someone to buy something, it can substantially improve your profitability. So how about suggesting a bit of that yummy fruit cake?

'Two coffees please dear.'
'Certainly, and why not try a bit of my yummy fruit cake? Freshly baked this morning.'
'Well, we're trying to watch our weight, my love.'
'Go on, spoil yourself. It's so light that we have to put a plate on it to stop it floating away.'
'Oh, go on then, just a small bit though.'

A PIECE OF CAKE

There you are, the first sale that is completely down to you. You asked the customers to buy, and dealt instinctively with their objections, then you persuaded them to spend at least double what they intended to and made them walk away smiling, happy and more than willing to repeat the experience. What more do you want?

I am sure that there are those of you out there who have no intention whatsoever of opening any sort of shop. It may even be the case that as an embryonic high-powered international business consultant, you feel that at the highest possible corporate level it may be a bit naff to offer a bit of fruit cake. Possibly, but even at these heady heights, the laws of selling, just like the laws of gravity, apply and are irrefutable. If you don't ask people to buy things, then they are very much less likely to buy.

IF YOU CAN'T GET A YES, THEN GO FOR A NO

An American colleague of ours not only does the guru bit, but also owns and manages a financial investment company. The products are sold on a purely cold basis, and because of this, they are quite expensive and complicated, and the success rate is quite limited – lucrative, but limited. He calculated that if his salesmen saw 100 people, they would sell 3 investments. While this made him loads of wonga, he felt that 97 potential customers were slipping through the net, and that the hit rate could be improved.

He looked at his salespeople's call records, and sure enough, amongst the 97 per cent were plenty of our now notorious 'v. int's.' For the sake of maths, we'll say that his team received £200 for a sale. This meant that 100 visits would yield £600. He decided to do something that on the face of it seems very strange indeed. He offered his salesforce the usual £200 a sale, but with the added, if not bizarre, incentive of £10 for a refusal. In other words, the 'yes' could bring in £600 for the salesperson, but the 'nos' could earn £970.

You may initially think that everyone who didn't buy was a 'no', but the no had to be a firm no, and in writing. To the salespeople's surprise, the nos were almost as hard to get as the yesses, but more than that, the results were fascinating: 12 yesses, 34 nos, and heaven only knows what the rest were doing. They were still 'v. int's', I suppose. Notice how the yesses were quadrupled simply because, instead of letting the customer drift along as a 'v. int', a decision was firmly asked for.

I know you will be a bit touchy on your first few client meetings, or when your first customers sidle in, but remember that if they don't buy, you starve. These examples may seem a little crude, and they are, but to start with, never forget to ask people to buy something.

YOU MAKE YOUR OWN LUCK

I can feel an uncomfortable shuffling out there, as you realize that you can't buy those half-moon spectacles, an apron, and live in a quaint workshop where hordes of happy, skipping children wait in joyful anticipation for your next hand-carved wooden toy.

As the realization dawns that you make your own luck as you make your own sales, I tend to get the 'high-pressure' defence hurled at me, which seems to suggest that high-pressure selling is not nice. I am nice, therefore I can't do high-pressure selling, therefore I shall starve with honour. Fine, if starving is your bag, but first tell me what high pressure is. It is very easy to dismiss the sales and marketing process as high pressure, but when pushed, people find it very difficult to define clearly what they mean by it.

SELLING IS CHILD'S PLAY

The two most popular definitions are, 'Pushy, won't take no for an answer', and perhaps more serious, 'Selling things to people that they don't want or need'. Let's deal with the first one.

I saw someone the other day who most certainly would not take no for an answer. They went on and on until their intended victim caved in, and yet after the event, they ended up loving each other. Do I detect a note of disbelief? OK, perhaps I should have explained that the person doing the persuading was about six years old.

> 'Dad, can I have a lolly?'
> 'No.'
> 'Why not?'
> 'Because you won't eat your tea.'
> 'If I promise I'll eat my tea, can I have a lolly?'
> 'No.'
> 'Why not?'
> 'Because your mother would kill me?'
> 'Mummy doesn't have to know. If I promise I'll eat my tea and I won't tell Mummy, then can I have a lolly?'
> 'Well perhaps a fruity one.'
> 'But I want a Chocolate one.'

I am sure you can see where this is going. We all had that ability once, but I suppose we lack the single-minded focus a kid has, and our good manners, along with the shyness adulthood has brought us, prevent us from doing that. Not that I am suggesting that the six-year-old's method works 'as is', or there again, maybe it does.

> 'Sir Nigel.'
> 'What?'
> 'Can I have the contract to supply your company with international investment advice?'
> 'No.'
> 'Why not?'
> 'Because I am not sure you could do it.'
> 'If I could prove I could do it...'

I know this is stretching your credibility a bit, but it isn't quite as daft as you may initially think. Firstly, consider in the real world what you would currently do if you were granted an opportunity to speak with Sir Nigel.

He opens up with 'What have you got to show me?' and you reply with 'Well Sir Nigel, I would just like to take this opportunity to introduce ...' (for the sake of brevity, we will remove the next two hours of nerve-driven gabble) '... and so, Sir Nigel, since I had the operation, playing the cello has been a lot less painful.'

Sir Nigel is slumbering gently but wakes with a start when he realizes you have finished. 'Ah well, yes, thank you for that. Have you any details you could leave me? Jolly good, I'll just see you out. I'm sure we will be in touch if we need anything,' and you will write 'v. int'. At least the six-year-old's approach asked for something, even if the initial answer was no. Anyway, even the no is useful because it is something to get our teeth into, a reason *why* he won't.

Watch what the kid does next. He investigates the reason for the no. When he is clear on it, he doesn't just offer a solution, he demands a deal for the solution. Commitment from the customer (his dad): 'If I promise to, then will you?' We'll do a bit on negotiating later, but this is a classic. The customer is only being offered the promise on condition that he proceeds. 'If we could manage a slightly better price, then could you give us the order today?'

You see, then, that this so-called childlike approach is actually a very powerful, if somewhat simple, first step to winning substantial business. I am afraid that you must also see from the £10 for a no story that even hardened pros lose the bottle to just come right out and ask for it. I suppose it is a fear of rejection and the fear that if the approach has too much brass neck, then it will put the customer off for life. While that may be true with aggressive or abrasive approaches, it does suggest that not taking no for an answer is a description of a poor technique.

I WISH I COULD BE THERE FOR YOU

Actually, it is a shame that this is only a book because a new enterprise is such an exciting prospect, I really wish I could be there with you for those first few vital weeks. I am sure together we would soon get those sales pouring in.

The second high-pressure thingy we considered was selling things to people that they did not want. Well, let me tell you right now: whatever you are selling, I don't want it. I am sure you will gasp at this and cry out 'But how can you say you don't want what I am selling when you don't know what I am selling?' Precisely. I DON'T KNOW WHAT YOU ARE SELLING, so how could I possibly want it?

There are companies all around the world that produce millions of things that you don't want, but it doesn't matter because it would take you five lifetimes just to hear about them, let alone to fill your normal working hours with unrequited desire for their products. It therefore stands to reason that we are starting from the position that we will initially be selling things to people that they don't want, because if we wait for people to find us, and subsequently discover they want us or our product, we are back to the lonely woman at her kitchen table waiting for people to find her and ask her to ice a cake.

Even if we offer a product that is an everyday one, the irony may be they still won't WANT it, for all sorts of reasons. Try making washing powder.

'No.'
'Why not?'
'Never heard of you/too cheap/too dear/I have got sensitive skin/we are happy with the one we use at the moment.'

And so on and on and on. We have to make them want it and that is going to take some effort.

WHAT ARE YOU SELLING?

They don't want what you are selling. What are you selling? Don't say soap powder because I am readying that old pig's bladder again. One of the oldest and most cheesy rib-ticklers in the marketing guru's repertoire is 'If you had a factory that manufactured drill bits, what would you sell?' To which the uninitiated would reply,

'Drill bits.' At this point our marketing genius starts to caper hysterically in ever-decreasing circles crying gleefully, 'No, no, no, you don't sell drill bits, you must sell them holes.' Stupid though this may appear, it is horribly right. Imagine you need to put up some shelves and you don't have the right sized drill. You set off to your local DIY store, and there is a stand displaying a revolutionary new product – 'self-adhesive holes'. All you need to do is select the size you require, peel off the backing paper, stick it on and bingo, you have a hole. You would never buy a drill again.

One of the loony business-speak activities that large companies indulge themselves with is setting up focus groups, which are teams of surplus executives that sit around examining their own navels and focusing on things. One of the favourite and slightly more useful 'things' is to consider the question, 'What business are we in?'. The answer often generates the considerably less useful bit of hilarity that is known as a mission statement. For example, a bank may start off by thinking drills. This would lead them to say they were in the banking business which means storing and lending money, but by thinking holes they could generate the mission statement: 'We are here to keep what you value safe, and to help you own the things you desire today instead of having to wait until tomorrow'.

As a mission statement, it makes me a little bilious, but the sales fraternity have made it their own by renaming it 'the opening benefit statement'. In other words, you don't walk up to someone and say, 'Do you want a loan,' because you get the answer 'no.' You say, 'Could you use a little extra cash?'

I got hijacked on the radio the other day because I sometimes earn a penny or two training salespeople, and the media feel I can be the representative high-pressure salesman to be pilloried to entertain their listeners, viewers, and readers. In this case I had come on the phone-in to answer questions on how to promote one's business, and the presenter sprung this little trap. He had found an old press cutting in which I had rather foolishly claimed that you could sell anything to anyone. Producing a small candle, he invited me to sell it over the air, and without telling anyone what it was, I had to get the highest price.

I promoted a source of mellow warmth and light that was totally self-contained and independent of any outside energy source. No matter what else lets you down, this could be depended upon to bring light, heat and happiness, with the reliability that could only be expected from a product so well designed that it had no moving parts whatsoever. We got offers of £25 and rising so fast that it shocked even me as to what people will buy, and I put a stop to it. And, if I had said do you want a candle?

Can you now see that what you are selling is not your product or service, but what it brings to your customer? That opening benefit thing I referred to means that our traditional oily salesperson will actually launch himself at you with what he has been told his product will do for you.

> 'Ah, hello, thank you for sparing me your valuable time. I just want to ask you if you would like to save money while protecting your loved ones from worry and upset at a time when they need to be protected from such things.'

Yep, he is flogging you an easy-payment funeral plan. You can adapt this technique, remove the sliminess, and tone it down to fit your personality and suit your business. Here are some examples:

'Go on, cheer yourself up and have one of our double-scoop chocolate fudge ice creams.' (An ice cream parlour.)

'Well, to save you the worry, we can organize that.' (A business consultant.)

'Firstly, let this book insure a good income for you and a joyous worry-free future.' (Me!)

NEVER TOO PROUD TO SELL SOMETHING

Those honest artisans amongst you often get all twitchy about the dismal standard of living that they have in relation to their skill compared to the income the fly-by-night double-glazing salesmen seem to be able to generate. It is often this differential and the desire to have one's skill valued that drives people into self-employment. It is then very sad to see the disillusionment when the skilled person finds that their skill has no greater value in self-employment than it did in their day job. If this has happened to you, the preceding bits should have started to give you a clue. Again, I ask you, what are you selling?

A lady on one of our sessions was the best seamstress and tailor that I have ever seen. The quality of her work was breathtaking. Her pricing was low, verging on the pathetic, and although she worked from home, it wasn't surprising that she had quite a few customers. She appeared one day looking a bit shocked. Apparently one of her customers she hadn't seen for a bit turned up very upset in a suit that looked as though it had been made for Quasimodo.

'What on earth happened to you?' she asked.

'Well,' the customer replied very sheepishly, 'I needed a suit for my son's graduation ceremony, and as it was such a special occasion I decided to go to a proper tailor.'

Now who's fault was that? I know you say that it was the stupid customer for failing to recognize real skills when he saw them, but I am going to suggest that it was the seamstress's fault for failing to sell something.

The something that I refer to is the surrounding magic. If I ran a tailor's shop, I would assume my best Italian accent and twiddle my moustache whilst offering freshly brewed cappuccinos and the finest fashion magazines. I certainly would not take an old shoe-box lid and write in felt tip 'OAP alterations. Half-price Tuesdays'. The fact I know nothing about tailoring means nothing. I can employ loads of people who are good at tailoring for a pittance. I know the secret of selling the magic, a much rarer and more valuable skill, and one I suggest you get stuck into right now.

POINTS TO PONDER

1 You won't go far wrong if you believe that everyone in the world can become your customer.

2 The simplest and most important rule is to ask people to buy something. When you part company, always ask yourself, 'Did I ask them to buy?'

3 Very interested isn't. Write that on your business wish list and the only person you fool will be yourself.

4 Although not subtle, the numbers game is not a bad place to start. The more people you ask, the more will buy.

5 Don't be afraid to be boring. Remember, your future security depends on it.

6 The simplest and most basic of sales technique can multiply profits beyond your wildest dreams.

7 If you want to know about persuasion and persistence, watch a child.

8 Get to know what you are really selling and what business you are really in.

9 Sell the magic and value of your enterprise to ensure a high income.

7

How Can You Sell Them Anything if You Can't Get to See Them?

In my previous book, *Resistance is Useless*, which is purely about persuasion and selling skills, I tried to illustrate the technique of 'selling people things they don't want' by imagining that we were selling a chieftain tank to Genghis Khan.

The theory was that, as a mediaeval warlord involved in a major battle, a tank from the 20th century would be invaluable to him. But when we ring him (on the mobile of course), we find that the 'Sorry to bother you squire, but I suppose you're not interested in a tank?' approach doesn't work. Firstly, I suppose that because he's a mediaeval warlord, he hasn't the foggiest idea what a tank is. So in the 'what are we selling' game, we decide to ring Genghis and offer 'Bloody slaughter, Mr Khan, death and destruction on a level that even you can't imagine. Mountains of skulls and rivers of blood.'

This is raw, unrefined stuff, and we are also making some very dangerous assumptions about Genghis's personality based on our preconceived prejudices of Mongol warlords. He may be a gentle type who is riddled with angst about his role as destroyer of the world. If we found that out, we could still sell the tank, but we would point out that when his stone-hurling, arrow-shooting and spear-chucking opponents see his fire-breathing, iron-clad machine, they will pack up and go home, thereby avoiding any unpleasantness. To dodge the misdirection by prejudice, we must do a bit of fact-finding, but that comes later.

During my construction of the Genghis story, another very important point was picked up. Setting aside all the 'rivers of blood' stuff, when we ring Genghis, what is the thing that we are setting out to sell to him in the first instance? In fear of my pig's bladder, I know you will now say 'victory over his enemies' or 'world domination', but the answer is a little more prosaic than that. The truth is that before we can start this benefit jiggery-pokery, we have got to get ourselves in front of the customer. In the case of Genghis, we must get an appointment to see him.

So, here you are. You have just been made redundant from 'Tanks International'; you have read this fabulous book by some ageing hippy on how to Go It Alone, and you have set up 'Jones's Warlike Solutions' in your back bedroom. Now what? You are far too honourable, despite the shabby way in which you were treated, to pinch anything from your old employer, so using your photographic memory and not their photocopier, you memorize the entire client list. Well, they are not going to come and see you, so you'd better go and see them. How?

You pick the name Genghis Khan off the list (mind you, I must say that your old company would have done better if they had kept their database up to date), and you decide to ring him. Tanks, cakes, consultancy or contract gardening: why are you ringing the potential customers? 'To sell them something,' you reply. No. People do not buy things on the phone. It is one of the biggest mistakes that I see my fledgling business chums make. I suppose the start of the disaster comes from so many sales gurus calling the discipline involved 'telephone selling'. Let's listen in on a typical call:

'ERE, DO YOU WANT TO BUY A TANK?

Ring, ring. 'Thank you for calling Consolidated Conkers. I'm Marianne, how may I help you?'
'Oh yes, I am Frank Jones and I have just set up a bit of a business, well sort of selling tanks and other stuff, and I wonder if anyone there is the right person to speak to about them?'

Good speech – you nearly sold their telephonist a tank – NOT. Now it is oily salesman time again. You have to get an appointment. You don't just find this bit hard because you are inexperienced, but because, in fact, this bit genuinely is hard. So hard in fact that our oily chums devote great swathes of their seminars to it. Receptionists are like gatekeepers, which makes them sound like slathering blood beasts or two-headed dogs which, I suppose, in some cases isn't that far off the mark. These people have been on similarly intense training programmes to learn how to keep people away from their lords and masters, even if it means burning you to a crisp with their fiery breath or shredding you with a single slash of their claws. With this in the mind of all experienced salespeople, the penetration of their defences is undertaken with some caution.

You will be faced with a series of questions that act as stoppers, such as 'Who is calling please? What company are you from? What is it concerning?' To the uninitiated, this tends to provoke a hurried description of themselves and their product. What good does that do? Do you really think she is going to say 'Oooh, yes, Sir Nigel would love one of those, you had better rush round and see him. Don't forget to bring a nice fat invoice.' I should co-co! What you actually get is 'Ye-e-e-ess, well, we are not looking for suppliers at the moment and Sir Ni-Gel is very busy, but if you would like to put some details in the post, I shall pass them on (to the waste compactor).'

If we look at this as a war, or a game, the classic management technique is to break the affair into three clear steps:

1 There is the objective – in this case to flog something to Sir Nigel which is tantamount to winning this war.
2 There is the strategy, which is how you plan before opening fire, based on the knowledge that experience and reconnaissance has brought.
3 Tactics. These are the methods that you bring to bear at each changing moment in the heat of battle.

The point that I am trying to make is while you may be fixed on your objective, don't let it interfere with your tactics for winning the individual skirmishes. In this case we have to get past Cerberus at the gate to meet the 'decision maker' as salespeople like to call the El Supremo (often wrongly, but that isn't for now). The first rule is that you must remember that the gatekeeper will not care that you make the best jam sponges in the world, or could even save their company millions. They are there to stop you wasting their boss's time, full stop. Keep it short, keep it simple. If you don't know who deals with your area of concern, the two-call strategy helps:

> 'Thank you for calling Thunderbolt Systems. I'm Ron, how may I help you?'
> 'Oh yes, who is responsible for jam sponge purchasing there?'
> 'Sir Nigel Caruthers, but ... '
> 'Thank you, ta ta.'

If you have decided to be that brief, it is not a bad idea to leave things for a day or two, in case they spot that the charming but icy cool international executive on the phone is the same rude pillock who rang up about 10 seconds ago.

I am in a bit of a quandary here because, from this point in, our oily chum will try to lubricate past on a glistening excretion of greasy charm. Certainly not for the inexperienced, the squeam-ish or the weak of stomach. However, without some of the more barefaced techniques, we are going to stay outside in the cold. So, take the following, but with a huge health warning and bear in mind how grim it can sound in the hands of an experienced salesperson, let alone a sincere beginner who is handicapped with the added burden of a conscience.

ALL THE WAY IN

You have got the guy's name, so ring up, but do not ask 'Could I speak to Sir Nigel please?' because they can just say 'No,' but if you ask 'Is Sir Nigel there?' then they are unlikely to lie. If he isn't there, just ask when he will be, and ring back then. If he is there and the gatekeeper says 'Yes,' this is a good start and a casual 'Oh good, put me through to him would you?' sometimes does the trick, but you must be prepared to deal with 'May I tell him who is calling?' and now we start a jolly game.

'It's Geoff,' is worth a try because it may be assumed that I am a chum, and be put through. 'Geoff who?' – oh well, not this time. 'Geoff Burch,' 'From?' That 'from' means 'What company are you from?', and any receptionist worth their salt won't fall into that old trap, but if they do, we reply with our home town 'Birmingham'. 'May I tell him what it is about?' By causing this delay, it is hoped that their switchboard is lighting up like a Christmas tree and they are coming under pressure to move you on. A number of sales gurus suggest that the whole thing can be toppled over the edge by a long-winded and incomprehensible explanation. If you make toothpaste you might say, 'I wish to discuss quasi-pharmaceutical dental maintenance products with special reference to his concerns over the erosion of the gingival fringe.' At this, you apparently should remain silent whilst what you have just said sinks in.

You have probably noticed from my tone that I appear sceptical. Maybe I am, but for some people these techniques work. My problem is that they scare the hell out of me and I can't always summon up the confidence to make them work for me.

IF THEY HATE YOU ENOUGH, THEY MAY AGREE TO SEE YOU (IF ONLY TO CUT YOUR THROAT)

Another good lever to use is to have a reason to call. I remember years ago watching an American cold-call sales superstar (that is what it is called by the way, a cold call, as opposed to a hot lead). He was addressing a huge sales conference on the skills required to make cold calls, and his party piece was to toss a telephone directory out into the audience and get someone to pick a name at random. He would then, live on stage, endeavour to make an appointment with the victim. The whole grisly spectacle was played over the auditorium's PA system. The first couple of calls got no answer, then someone picked up the phone:

> 'Oh hi there Sir, my name is J.B.J. Sheckenberger the 17th and I would like this opportunity to introduce the Acme Life Plan to you.'
>
> The response was just a little unexpected. 'Acme, Acme! How dare you ring me. It is your company that has brought tragedy and misery on my whole family and you have the nerve to call me.'

The audience realized that the demonstration had gone horribly wrong and prepared to watch an entertainment rarely enjoyed since the Romans stopped feeding people to lions, but our hero barely broke step.

> 'Gee Sir, I heard that you were upset and that really breaks me up, and that's why I have to come and see you so that I can sort this out for you and find out just why you are so disappointed.'

It wasn't long before he had made an appointment with this guy, which is of course only what he had promised he could do at the start. Who knows what reception was waiting for him if he had shown up, but that wasn't the problem. The moral of that tale is if you have got something to hang your hat on, making appointments can be that bit easier.

A less dramatic and nerve-wracking example with which you may feel more comfortable is the use of the published lists of contract winners. Particularly in the building trade, you can purchase the names of companies, developers and architects that have won projects. This means that you can ring up and say 'Is Nigel in ...' and so on, and when asked 'What is it concerning?' you reply, 'It is about his worries with the truss structure on the Washington job.' The point is that as this is their big new project, the mention of it should set the gatekeeper's alarm bells ringing enough to realize that it may not be clever to obstruct the progress of this job.

Even after all of this, when you get through to El Supremo, you have still got to persuade him to give you an appointment.

TOO BUSY FIGHTING THE WAR

In the Genghis Khan skit that I did, from what I remember, I based it on one of the classic oiliest of oily techniques:

'Mr Khan, if you could spare just a few minutes of your time, I am sure ...'

'I am too busy, I've got a war to fight.'

'I understand that Mr Khan, but if I could demonstrate that our war machine could win that war, wouldn't it be worth investing a few minutes to discover the benefits of ...'

'Send me details.'

'I would love to, but this machine has to be seen to be believed, and I would be prepared to show it ...'

'You would be wasting your time.'

'Mr Khan, I am prepared to risk a few minutes to show you how to gain victory if you are.'

'I am skint.'

'That, Mr Khan, is why it would be worth discussing with me how our new 'Bloody Slaughter Pay-as-You-Pillage' lease scheme can help you.'

'I am happy with the arms supply people I have got at the moment.'

'And so you should be Mr Khan. A successful warlord such as yourself would not have laid waste half the known world without a reliable supply of weapons, but I am sure you will agree, you didn't achieve your unparalleled success by not investigating dramatic advances in weapon design that could change the whole future of warfare.'

'Look, it sounds very interesting, but I have a war to fight so send me details.'

'OK, Mr Khan, could I have your details? Where are you at present?'

'Outer Mongolia.'

'Outer Mongolia? Never! That's on my way home! Let me drop the details off to you and as I am taking the transporter home tonight, I will have a tank on board you can have a look at.'

That lot is more or less text-book perfect, and if you have the bottle to carry it off, you are a better person than I, because it scares me.

TOO SCARED TO BE CONFIDENT

When I first started my consultancy, we had to get customers fast, so we had to make appointments. Everyone I rang made the Khan seem approachable and even-tempered. At this point, things can get very depressing. It is all very well reading smart-arsed, upbeat books like this, but when you are out there amongst the blood and the bullets being told to 'Get stuffed' at every phone call, it's kind of hard to see the point, especially as the precious bank balance turns into whacking great overdraft before your very eyes. But this is where you must redouble the effort. I cannot stress how important this is.

Of all the enterprises that come to me to say they have failed, the biggest cause is lack of work. Even when they give different reasons such as cash flow, or prices forced too low, underneath is still a lack of work. If you had more customers than you knew what to do with, you would pick the ones that pay most and pay quickest. If you are confident that your product or service is the very best on offer, and your prices are spot on, then we can work on the lack of work thing.

The thing that excites me most about this book is that, if we can get things right together, success for you will become inevitable, but you must gather the confidence to go out there and make it happen for you. We are no different from each other. I find ringing huffy strangers who are likely to tell me to take a hike just as daunting as you do, but once through that barrier, the future is assured. To start with, I became unnerved by my lack of success and started a sort of dismal chain reaction which meant that the knocks I was taking made me use an even more disaster-prone approach: 'Er, um, hello. I don't suppose you are interested in training at the moment?'

The 'no' was quick and short, and it meant I could vanish into the mist. However, it wasn't exactly getting things off to a flying start.

MEET JOHNNY KAMINSKI

A friend had come round to try and help. At mid-morning we had had enough and stopped for a coffee, a cake and a whinge. 'I wish we had one of those flash American salespeople to help,' my buddy said wistfully. I agreed and we fantasized about how this American hero would gallop to our rescue, Lone Ranger style. With his six guns of great techniques blazing, he would cut through the crap and get us all the appointments we could use. We decided that he would wear a blazer and slacks, have a smile that twinkled like a toothpaste ad, be well tanned and called Johnny Kaminski.

Things went a little too far and, during a rush of blood to the head, I decided to employ the talents of the said Johnny Kaminski. Putting on my most ludicrous American accent, I started to ring potential clients:

'Acme Bearings.'
'Woah, hi there, my name's Johnny. May I ask you your first name?'
'Oh, er, um, Carol.'
'Well hi there Carol, it's real nice to speak with you. Tell me, is Mr Jackson there right now.'
'He is, but he is rather busy, can I ask what it is about?'
'Sure you can Carol. The fact is that I have a great opportunity for him, and I know he wouldn't want to miss it … Hi there Mr Jackson. Great of you to speak to me right away. Sure, I'll

tell you why I'm ringing. Mr Jackson, I'm ringing you because I have just got to come and see you.'

'What about?'

'WHAT ABOUT! Hoo, hot dog! Mr Jackson, I have got just the greatest opportunity for you. No way can I discuss this on the phone. I am just so darned excited for, Mr Jackson, you are going to be so happy. Look, how about tomorrow at 10 minutes to 10, or would the next day be better?'

I know that at this moment you are feeling nauseous and you are declaring that you would put the phone down on someone like that. The scary thing is that people didn't. Johnny Kaminski's strident, driving style against all the tenets of good taste and my better judgement was able to put the hit rate through the roof. One minor drawback was that we couldn't keep the appointment because it was hard enough being my Atlantic alter ego on the phone, and it would have been truly impossible face to face. I wasn't too sure how cheery the welcome would be either, which is one of the drawbacks of aggressive appointment making, but there again, it is not as big a drawback as not making appointments at all.

JOHNNY'S TRICKS

By the way, Johnny used a couple of quite keen little wrinkles as well. He suggested 10 to the hour as a time, the theory behind this being that the client (wrongly) deduces the interview will be brief (10 minutes in fact). He may look at his diary and see appointments on the hour or even half hour but not in between. Johnny then offered a choice. This is the classic alternative close. The customer is completely free to choose whether to do business with you, or to do business with, er, well you, actually. Instead of our traditional, 'Did you want one or not?', where 'not' is a choice, or 'Did you want anything else?', where 'No thanks, I'll have my bill' is the choice, we offer 'Did you want the red or the green?', 'Ten to ten, or ten to eleven?', or 'Did you want pudding, or just coffee?'.

The real lesson with Johnny Kaminski, though, is one of confidence. Whether you liked his style or not, he did, and he believed in it to the point where he could run faster than a speeding train, leap high buildings in a single bound, and make appointments with anybody. If you are going to succeed at this lark, you must be the equal of anybody, and if you are ringing someone to allow them to share in the good fortune of your miracle talents, don't be apologetic. Whatever you offer, be it a tea shop, house cleaning or atomic physics, it will compete with the best in the world because that has to be your aspiration, and if that is what you offer, do it boldly.

My chum with the fabric shops has such belief in himself that on all his press adverts he puts in bold letters the warning, 'Be prepared to queue'. When your clients are prepared to queue, then you have cracked it.

POINTS TO PONDER

1 First and foremost, by hook or by crook, get face to face with your customer.
2 Do not try to sell over the phone, especially to your customers' receptionists.
3 Receptionists and secretaries are trained to keep you out, therefore you will need to train yourself before you get in.
4 Remember your goal, and that is simply to get in and talk to whom you want to talk to.
5 If you have no excuse to call them, create one. Even if it doesn't appear positive at first, anything that gives a reason to talk is good.
6 Johnny's confidence is what carried him through. People are overwhelmed by confidence so develop some now.

8

OK, So Now You're In, Then What?

Now we have got the customer in front of us, it might be a good idea to ask them to buy something, but what?

People in my groups starting out on this rocky road say 'If only I could get in to see Sir Nigel, all my troubles would be over'. Or, 'It's a closed shop. If they would just give me a few minutes to put my case, I would be made'. OK, with a cheery wave of my magic wand, I whisk you into the presence of the client of your dreams. NOW WHAT?

What are you going to do? There is a thing that American school children indulge in, apart from sleep-over parties and shooting each other, and that is 'show and tell' lessons, where a child brings in a thing of interest, maybe a hobby model or what have you. They then proceed to 'show it' to the class, and 'tell' their chums all about it. I tell you this simply to ask you, is that what you wanted the appointment for? It might be worth stating that the American kid has no desire to actually flog his model to the class, and if he did, it would be the worst way of doing it.

This valuable opportunity must not be wasted on show and tell. You meet with the customer with a view to getting something for yourself. When I ask people who are just off to see clients, 'Why are you going to see them, what are you going to ask for, and what do you hope to get?', the answer is often just a bewildered silence. It is a great wonder to me that people can open their shop or restaurant or visit potential clients without knowing why.

WHERE AM I? WHAT AM I DOING HERE?

In my sales-coaching days, I would go out on a one-to-one basis with various less-than-eager victims, whose employers felt they needed a little healthy encouragement. We would stop outside a call and I would say 'What are we doing here?' Perhaps we can get the spectre of this book to haunt you in the same way I would haunt my trainees. We have got that appointment, the one you always wanted, and it is tomorrow. Now what do you expect to get from it, and why are you going? Someone walks into your tea shop. Why are they there, and what will you ask them to buy? If you can consider these questions, you will take a great step forward because just having that awareness the whole time you are with a customer will massively improve your success rate.

Another helpful wheeze is to develop a regular checklist. Every profession or pursuit where the outcome is important or even fatal tends to use checklists. Pilots, parachutists, surgeons – they all check through their equipment and procedures to ensure success is repeated each time. For an airline pilot, success means bumbling cheerfully into passport control and not being carried in bits contained in various plastic bags off a Peruvian mountainside. If that little comment raised your eyebrows a bit, remember it isn't that much fun going bust either, so let's develop our pre-flight and post-flight checks.

Post-flight first, I think. I have a four-point checklist, which is as follows:

1 What did I achieve? Have I secured my objective?
2 What information have I gathered that will be of use to me in future dealings with this client?
3 What information have I gathered that will be of use to me with finding and keeping other clients?
4 If I did this one again, what would I have done better?

I would like you to write down these four points and carry them about with you. I still do it, and it brings consistently reliable results. There is so much to say about each point that I will deal with them one at a time. Points one and two are covered in this chapter, and points three and four are discussed in Chapter 9.

Imagine you have just made the momentous first visit to your potential customer. What would be the first question on your checklist? I would suggest the following:

1 WHAT DID I ACHIEVE? HAVE I SECURED MY OBJECTIVE?

This one is a cracker because achieving your objective implies that you actually had an objective in the first place. This is going to be very tricky to write about because we are going to try and translate 'seat of the pants', gut-feeling stuff into gritty, practical steps. Perhaps we should invent a case study to help understanding.

You have set up a company to undertake catering for special corporate events, and you know that Thunderbolt Leisure PLC is a really big player when it comes to entertaining their clients. Well go on then, get started. I'll give you a hand if you get stuck.

Returned to Sender

Write them a nice letter? Ring them? Nice letters don't tend to work that well, but it is not a bad idea to write and then ring. Who are you going to write to and ring? I know, someone at Thunderbolt, but who? Perhaps a bit of telephone research would help:

> 'Thank you for calling Thunderbolt Leisure PLC. I'm Suzy, how may I help you?'
> 'Oh, yes, thank you very much. Could you tell me who is responsible for all your corporate hospitality?'

Our gatekeeper gets about seven zillion salespeople every day doing something similar, so be prepared for:

'I think it would be our Mr Jones, but he is very busy at the moment and...'

'It's OK, thank you, I'll call back later.'

We've been through all that, so we will assume that your fault-less charm and rapier wit has secured that appointment. Why are you going to see him? If you say 'to introduce myself to him', remember my lurking pig's bladder. You want his business. Currently he is giving £50,000 worth of business to someone inferior to you. (If you think that was a bit arrogant, and if you are inferior to his current supplier, don't waste your telephone bill ringing him.) You have to get in there and take that business. When the buyer discovers that he is much better off doing business with you, he will be thrilled.

This better off, superior stuff may be unsettling you a bit, but you had plenty of time in previous chapters to sort this out. I am desperate for you to succeed, prosper and win enough business to support the lifestyle of your dreams, but if what you offer is crap, then you will only beat those who are crappier. What upsets me is those of you who are superior in every way and still go bust because you failed to communicate that to the potential customer.

In the Hot Seat

Here we sit then, in front of Mr Jones. We want his business, but is our range what he wants, are our prices what he can afford, is our trading style what he is looking for? Maybe we should talk at length about our range, our prices and our trading style until our intended victim becomes so bored that he submits to our demands through fear of dying of fatigue. 'Ho, ho, ho,' you guffaw at my rib-tickling little japes, then why oh why when I go around with people do they adopt the aforementioned tactic with absolutely no sense of irony.

The Gift of the Earhole

When people accuse me, somewhat abusively I think, of being a 'good salesman', I feel obliged to ask them why they think so, and they then go on further to accuse me of some mysterious affliction called the 'gift of the gab'. I may hold my hands up to the first charge of being a 'good salesman', and even to the second, but I assure you they don't go together. Persuasiveness is a listening skill. It is the 'gift of the earhole'.

Some bright spark, while trying to illustrate this concept, suggested that nature made us natural salespeople by giving us one mouth and two ears to remind us that, when selling, we should listen twice as much as we talk. If nature had really constructed us to remind us of the correct ratio of listening to talking, we would have heads that looked like cheap swimming hats with about 2,000 ears all over them. The trick is to shut up and sell, which demands special questioning and listening skills.

Now back to the objective. May I suggest that the objective is 'to flog them something?'. Now when you come out of your meeting, instead of being all busy business speak with 'Did you achieve your objective?', I can ask you, 'Did you flog them anything?' To which you reply? Perhaps you feel I am being too coarse, brutal and up-front. You may feel that the first meeting was not the time to ask the intended victim to buy anything. So come on, answer me this: are you ever going to ask them to buy anything? Oh you are. When? 'When the time is right' is the usual cheery reply I receive. When is the time right? 'I don't know, but I'll know it when I see it.'

We can get ourselves into an astonishingly circular argument here. I will say that the time must come when you do ask for something, and you might say that as you were getting on so well with this new acquaintance it would be a pity to spoil it by asking them to buy something. So you would say that the time is never right. You would defend your position by arguing that my recommendation that you rush into an office, grab the person in charge by the lapels and haul them up until their face is milli-metres from yours and scream 'Buy now or it will be the worse for you pal,' is perhaps a touch intrusive. It may even be a tad counter-productive if you find yourself being carried back out into the street by security. There has to be a solution to this or we will either be battered to death by burly security guards, or spend our life and savings having endless, everlasting chats and meetings with new-found chums who never buy anything.

Well? How Are You Doing So Far?

Let's go back to our example. The guy in question has the control on £50,000 worth of business we would like. You visit him as we planned earlier, and I meet you outside afterwards:

> 'How did you get on?' I ask cheerfully.
> 'Very well,' you reply.
> 'So you got the 50 grand then?'
> 'Well not yet, but he is v. interested.'

I will suggest that the objective of this call was to secure that £50,000 worth of business. You may feel that this is a fairly steep requirement for a first meeting with such an important client so early in your business career, but then what on earth do we set as the objective? Half-way to getting the business, or even a quarter way? Tell me how you are going to know.

A great Zen teacher said, do not jump a chasm in two bounds (for obvious reasons). In my professional field, which is the job of ensuring the success of salespeople, the biggest problem is measuring that success. If after this initial call I ask 'Well, was that call a success?', what will you answer? 'I think so.' 'Why do you think so?' 'Well, he seemed very friendly.' This is an eternal problem in selling. If you are sawing through a piece of wood, you can see the whole time how far you have got, and if it is a narrow piece, it takes less time than a wide piece, but with a customer, not only do you not know how far you have got, you don't know how far you have got to go. By that I mean that there are different types of sale to make. The ones that concern us here are major sales and minor sales. For those of you readers who are opening the cafés, shops, window-cleaning rounds and so on, and have been feeling a teensy bit left out by all this, you can now join in again.

In the small sale, success is easy to measure. If you sell chocolate bars, or offer to clean windows, we must consider the commercial decision of the customer to be a small one (not unimportant you understand, but small). Let us have two defined score positions: SUCCESS and FAILURE.

Some People Wouldn't Know Success if it Bit Them on the Bottom

A man walks into our sweet shop and says 'Ere mush, how much are your choc bars?' You reply, 'They're 28p, Lord bless you, sir.' If he buys, that is a success. If he doesn't, then it can be construed as a failure. This can be expressed as SUCCESS = SELLING SOMETHING. FAILURE = NOT SELLING ANYTHING.

Before we get back to our £50,000 catering contract, I hope that the small-decision folk among you appreciate that not selling does equal failure. When they order a cup of coffee from you, you have failed if you don't ask them if they would like a slice of cake, and as buying a slice of cake could hardly be described as a major decision, you have failed if they don't buy one. If you wonder why a few quid here or there matters, let me explain how that is the key to all of this. It is the key to the major sale, and it is the key to obtaining huge riches beyond the wildest dreams of personal wealth.

A great guru – a Zen Buddhist or someone from the Macclesfield Chamber of Commerce, I can't recall – asked his followers how they should eat an elephant. The answer was 'a bit at a time'. I am told by new business start-ups that, way off in the future, they would like to own some fabulous luxury such as a Ferrari. To a jobbing window cleaner, that is a bit like eating an elephant. 'When do you want it?' I ask, a sly grin playing across my craggy features. 'I'd like it now of course, but if I could afford it next year, that would be great.' Let's see, shall we? You could get a real cracker of a Ferrari for £150,000. That means you'd have to put aside around £3,000 a week, that's about £75 an hour, or if you like, £1.25 a minute or about 2p a second, so while reading this you have just dropped about six quid out of your Ferrari fund.

I know this brings a kind of uncomfortable stark realization to the dream, but perversely it also makes it attainable. If you realigned your goal to a more realistic 10 years, that would mean putting around £7.50 an hour aside which wouldn't be that difficult, or you may decide after doing the sums that a red Italian sports car isn't worth the bother, but then that's the fun and pleasure of self-employment. It gives you the choice.

As with the Ferrari and the elephant, the route to success in the £50,000 job must be broken into *measurable*, bite-sized pieces. All we need to do now, before wending our merry way up the shining path to economic success, is to decide exactly how we define a major sale as opposed to a minor one, and once we have done that, how we measure our success.

The way we decide whether our enterprise is involved in the major sales process or not is not determined by the cash amount but by a series of other criteria. The person who wants an excuse for not selling on the day tends to put the failure down to the size of the sale, but in cash terms it doesn't hold water. A small boy investing a year's pocket money in a small bottle of perfume for his mum may be nearer to a major sale than an eastern potentate spending a few million on a whim to buy yet another executive jet because he likes the colour of the upholstery. A lady comes into your boutique and fancies a £750 coat. Offer to put it on the plastic and, bingo, the sale is yours. The real test of a major sale is a another little checklist that I like to run:

A. It Takes Time to Complete and Conclude the Sale Successfully
As with our £50,000 catering contract, it will take some time to complete the journey that results in us toddling off to the bank with the cheque for 50 grand. This doesn't mean that you can muck about taking too long over some minor decision and then call it a major decision because you lacked the bottle to ask for the business.

B. It is Unlikely that an Immediate Purchase Will Be Made
Again, what I mean is if you have genuinely done your utmost to secure the sale correctly and it is still obvious that you won't fulfil your objective on that day.

C. More Than One Sales Visit or Meeting is Required
(More of this in a moment.)

D. There is Often More than One Person Involved in the Buying Decision

It may be a board of directors or even a whole community and you need to convince them all. That might mean getting to see all of them. Our catering manager may say 'I love the way you have dealt with my problem and I shall put your proposal to my committee with my own recommendation.' You certainly would write 'v. int', but I hate to depress you: the chance is that this guy can't put over your unique point and the enthusiasm that you bring to your presentation. When he sees that he is screwing up and his committee are frowning in disapproval, he will back-pedal, and your valued 'v. int' soon becomes a less welcome 'up yours!'.

E. The Buyer is Cautious Because a Buying Mistake Would Have Major Repercussions

This, I suppose, is one of the more important measures. If you go back to the eastern potentate or the wealthy woman, neither of them cares if they become bored or disappointed with their purchases. The plane may be left to rot in the desert, or given to the airforce for training; the coat will hang at the back of the wardrobe and be forgotten. But should our contact choose the wrong caterers, he would fear the sound of the chairman in the dining room shouting 'Who's the idiot who changed our caterers?', or your own partner when you have bought a new home saying, 'Well there's no use you moaning, you wanted to live here.'

This is a particularly tricky point for us of the one-person-band persuasion because we are going to see buyers in companies and ask them to change from their possibly long-term, maybe large supplier to us. 'How long have you been offering a design and build service for atomic power stations?' 'Oh, over a week now' is a reply that tends to drain away buyer confidence.

To depress you yet more, it is possible that you have heard that your biggest target customer has been let down very badly by their current supplier, so as you should, you rush round there to offer yourself. After a few tough questions about where you heard about the troubles, you are welcomed like an old friend, and the whole turgid story is poured out to you. When you come away, you don't even bother to write 'v. int' because this is 'in the bag'. Then the phone doesn't ring and the order doesn't arrive. You phone to find out what is holding things up, only to discover to your amazement that they have decided to stay with their current supplier. I can feel the heat of your disbelief radiating from here, and I don't blame you. It is one of the most amazing phenomena I have ever encountered. I am going to have to be very careful here because I don't really want to be sued by anyone, but I must tell you about two completely true examples that recently happened to me.

We Are Quite Happy with the Robbing Lunatics We Use at the Moment, Thank You

If you think you recognize your own company from the following, be assured that it isn't you, and any similarity is purely coincidental.

One firm came to me in tears and said that they had commissioned a highly confidential attitude survey based on the company's most sensitive future plans. The consultancy involved produced a staff programme created uniquely, they said, from the data.

Some time later, a senior manager joined from the company's most bitter competitor. He brought with him all his documents (we are not discussing morals here), and to our lachrymose friends' absolute horror, here was this unique and confidential system, with just the names changed. The consultant had told both parties that he was exclusively working for them, and charged them both for the research, and put into the hands of a competitor the most sensitive market information.

I don't like distress purchases, especially where there is trouble and bad feeling, so I backed away. Six months later, I met the senior director who had approached me:

'What was the outcome?' I asked. 'Did you sue them, did you have them flogged, did you hire the Tongs to slaughter them and their families?'
'Well, we did appoint another consultancy, but then Charley [the baddy in all this] came to see us and he was very sorry and well, I think it was all a bit of a mix-up that got blown out of proportion, so we went back to him.'

Can you believe that? Are they mad?

Another company discovered that a long-term supplier was blatantly bribing buyers to get better terms. When this was discovered, the buyer was fired but the supplier got back in. I often add a touch of spice to my tales to pep them up a bit, but be assured that these two examples are the stone-cold truth.

'We Got the Business. Have We Failed?'

The only explanation I can give for this extraordinary behaviour is that people fear change, even from a bad situation. All that the bad suppliers proved was that suppliers can be untrustworthy and duplicitous; they have not proved that you aren't. In fact, the evidence provided by the previous supplier is that that is the nature of suppliers, of which you are one. Proving your credentials will become part of your sales presentation, but first we will get back to eating our elephant.

Perhaps we have decided what we are involved in is a major decision, as measured by the preceding criteria. We must now determine whether that initial call to our catering manager was a success or not. Remember where we started, as I rode with you to the first meeting. 'Why are you going to see this person?' I ask. 'What do you hope to come away with, and how can we judge this meeting a success?' Let's run just one possibility:

> Knock, Knock.
> 'Come in! What did you want to see me about?'
> 'Oh yes, begging your pardon your honour, I was led to believe that you put out 50 grand's worth of catering business.'
> 'If I do, what concern is it of yours, stout artisan?'
> 'Begging your pardon your worshipfulness, I wouldn't be lying if I told you that that business would do me a bit of alright, seeing as how I am in the catering trade and right good I am an' all, begging your pardon sir.'
> 'I admire your pluck, here's a cheque for £50,000. Start on Monday.'

Where do we place this one on the capricious seesaw of success and failure? It would be very churlish to call this anything less than a resounding success. On the other hand, if the guy says 'Out, out, out, and never darken my door again. If you are seen within three miles of this establishment I will have you shot,' I will tend to lean towards the failure side of things. Having said that, a reception like that makes me determined to sell to them, but then I am perverse and for now we'll leave the more challenging customers for another day.

It is starting to look as though the measure for a small sale and a large sale is the same: SALE = SUCCESS; NO SALE = FAILURE. We have agreed that we need to make more visits, so how was it after the first visit? They didn't buy but they didn't threaten to have us shot. What do we call that? Eureka! I know, we will call it 'v. int'.

The Ratchet Effect

You are going to hate me for this, but I am going to classify 'v. int' as failure because there is no positive result, and in any event, the situation is out of your control. What we are after is measurable progress towards our goal. I call it the 'ratchet effect' because, like a ratchet, every bit of activity results in a click – the reassuring noise that tells us that things cannot fall back to where we started from.

Back to our catering. I want to hear things like this:

'... so that is why I feel we can do a great job.'
'That is most interesting. Of course, my MD must be involved so let me speak to him and then by the end of the month I will call.'
'Have you got your diary handy?'
'Yes.'
'Well, look. Let me prepare some sample menus now I know what you want, and then I can present them to you and your MD. Would the 28th be OK, or would the 29th be more convenient?'

OK, you haven't left with the contract in your pocket, but you took the initiative and secured that next appointment which is a very big loud click from the ratchet. Be very careful that you don't form one of these cosy relationships where the other person is happy to see you because there is no danger of you asking them to buy anything. It just goes on forever with no result. That is a FAILURE.

Don't Be Afraid to Show it to the Foreman

The big flash sales books for the cognoscenti bang on about the vital importance of seeing the decision maker. It is this old chestnut of qualifying again. Obviously in certain respects they are correct: if, for example, the person you are talking to isn't authorized to sign cheques or make buying decisions, you are unlikely to get either from them. That being said, it is unrealistic for us to stride into our target company, see the person in charge, tell him quite firmly he is to buy from us or suffer the consequences and stride out with a cheque. With our ratchet effect, our first meeting doesn't have to be with the decision maker as long as the clicks on the ratchet take us that way. The rule is to invite each person you meet to take the maximum decision they are allowed to make. Accepted practice would say that it would be a waste of time to demonstrate a machine to a factory foreman, but not if, when you have impressed him, you ask him to arrange for his boss to attend the next demonstration. CLICK.

We move on up. Be warned: when you get back to your car, I will be waiting with my pig's bladder and our four-point checklist. I expect to see a written order, the money, or at the very least a firm appointment in writing, in your diary, for the next click. This will not include 'v. int, ring next week to touch base'. That is a FAILURE. Just to make it clear at the end of this section, number one on our list was DID I ACHIEVE MY OBJECTIVE? This is to provoke you on every contact with a customer to realize that you INTEND TO SELL. Whether it is a doughnut, extra onions, the opportunity to quote, or to flog a power station, your future livelihood depends on this determination.

To round this bit off, it is quite good to note that having an objective is also quite a good talisman against the Go-It-Aloners' biggest risks when hunting those first few clients, and that is the danger of ambush. I hope that after hearing the cautionary tale of the cake-icer you will agree that, despite your many skills and talents, we must go forth and capture those new clients.

Do Not Get Ambushed

A turgid but recognized sales method is to 'cold call'. The slang description which perhaps is more self-explanatory is 'on the knocker'. It involves traipsing around industrial estates or whatever, and arriving unannounced in the hope of doing some business. Often small companies have no one in reception, just a telephone or a frosted-glass hatch to bang on, if you dare, because by the phone and the hatch is a sign that says in bold letters 'NO REPRESENTATIVES SEEN WITHOUT AN APPOINTMENT', but it is worth a try anyway. Turgid it may be, but take my word, it can be worthwhile, especially if you have invested time and effort travelling to a specific appointment and find yourself in the area with time on your hands.

This, however, is where ambushes can happen. One strides, or rather creeps in, and rouses the thing behind the frosted glass in defiance of the dire warning about appointments. You would be right to anticipate being booted back out, perhaps with the consolation of some useful names and information, but on this occasion things are different:

'Who would deal with staff training?' you ask.
'Mr Roberts,' replies the thing.
'Is he in?'
'Yes.'
'Then may I see him please?'
'Who shall I tell him is calling.'
'My name's Geoff Burch.'
The thing picks up the phone: 'Mr Roberts, I have got a Geoff Brunch who does stiff trading,' and before you can get your hands round its throat, it says to your astonishment, 'He said he'll come out and see you if you would like to take a seat.'

This is where the ambush starts because, as you squat on a black vinyl seat that is a foot from the floor so you have no hope of rising with dignity, and browse nonchalantly through a 10-year-old copy of *Sewage Handling Technology* magazine, you will be offered a drink. 'Would you like a drink?' Do not accept because what you will receive is a thin plastic cup of boiling mud. Due to its blistering heat, you may just be able to hold it by hooking your fingernails to the rim while the scalding steam broils your palm. Of course, any attempt at actually drinking it is out of the question.

There we are then, knees around our ears, the drink in one hand while with the other we balance the magazine and act casual. Our potential customer explodes out of a door somewhere and thrusts out a hand. 'Name's Roberts. What have you got to show me?' The battle is already lost as you struggle to get up like one overturned woodlouse, all legs and a crotch full of boiling mud. The customer is impatient and is looking at his watch and tapping his foot even as this steaming, dishevelled heap rises to its feet before him. 'Make it quick, I've got a meeting. What have you got to show me?'

This is the ambush and it is useless to us. What will you do? Hop about trying to open your briefcase with one hand while wildly endeavouring to support it on the free knee? The briefcase, of course, resists every attempt at entry until it explodes like a yuletide novelty bomb, but instead of toys and entertaining novelties, it scatters papers, sandwiches and spare underwear to the four winds. The client's impatience has subsided to a contemptuous sneer. Partially reassembled, you gabble, 'Er, um, I've not been, um, but I have started providing er, well I'm sure you often, well, you know.' 'Well, thank you for that, I am sorry I can't spare you any more time, but if you leave me some details, I'm sure if we need it looking at, we'll be in touch.' With that he vanishes, and you write 'v. int'. Well he isn't 'v. int', and you cocked that up.

Be assured that no one will buy standing in a foyer, across the roof of a car in a car park, or in the corridor outside an office. A bit of gentle assertiveness is required here, so with that in mind, let's do some loin girding and say as soon as we see our client, 'Is there somewhere comfortable we can go and discuss this?' If the reply is 'Look, you've come bounding in here unannounced and I'm very busy. I've got a meeting in five minutes, so tell me what you've got to show me,' then say 'I'm so sorry to have disturbed you, obviously you don't have the time now, but can I use this opportunity to make a proper appointment with you?' It might not be a sale, but it is a big click on that ratchet.

At the moment that person is not our customer: he may hate us on sight, or tell us that he is happy with the people he is using at the moment. That is his present position. It is our job to move him from that position to one of 'Yes, yes, where do I sign? Would you like a bucket of cash now?' To do this successfully, we must choose the place and the pace. This is why it is inadvisable to accept the drink: our pace is not determined by us but by the cooling time of coffee. When the deal is done, the contract signed and you should be on your way, the client says 'Do stay and finish your drink,' so as you sit blowing on it and fanning it with your hat, he says:

'So, how long have you been in corporate security?'
'Um, about a week actually.'
'Really? Where did you get your qualification?'
'I did a course in prison.'

All because of a cup of coffee. What you must say when offered a drink is 'No thank you very much, I've not long had one. Now, shall we get down to business?' Nice solid control, I love it.

Knowledge is Power
Now to number two on our checklist, and one of the most vital elements of persuading anyone to do anything. As I lie in wait in your car with the pig's bladder at the ready, my second question will be:

2 WHAT INFORMATION HAVE I GATHERED THAT WILL BE OF USE TO ME IN FUTURE DEALINGS WITH THIS CLIENT?

This is a seminal moment because it is vital that you understand why you are seeing this customer. The classic answer is 'Well, to tell them a bit about me and my company.' In fact, the shrewd buyer that you are likely to meet is quite capable of saying, 'Very nice to meet you, do sit down. Now tell me a bit about you and your company.' My question to you is 'Why?' And, before you ramble off about giving the customer enough information to help them make up their mind, remember that lurking pig's bladder. Even you budding restaurateurs can cock things up here:

> 'What cakes do you have?'
> 'Well, we have apple turnovers, fruit cake, carrot cake, iced fancies, cattle cake, pancake, doughnuts, tea cake, buns, Victoria sandwich, ... [one hour later] wedding cake, cherry pie, Dundee cake ...'

All that you do is bore and confuse the customer. My hero Machiavelli clearly states that knowledge is power, so why are you giving your power in the shape of knowledge away?

What we want is knowledge from the customer, and the best way to do that is to learn the twin skills of asking questions and listening:

> 'What cakes do you have?'
> 'What cakes would you like?'

At this point you will plunge into one of the great controversies of selling. The battle rages amongst sales trainers not about whether questions are valid, because everyone agrees that they are, but about what type of questions to ask.

The 'Say No' Controversy

The cause of it all is the dollop that lumbers up to you in shops and says 'Can I help you?' and you say 'No, just looking.' This approach is deemed ineffective because the customer has this tendency to say no. This is not blamed on the fact that you were approached by a blank-eyed dismal assistant, but on the quality of the question in as much as it allows a yes or a no answer. In fact, there is one school of sales philosophy that calls it a 'say no question'.

There is an old playground game that requires you to rush up to a chum and say:

> 'I bet I can ask you something you can't say no to.'
> 'Go on then.'
> 'What's your name?'
> 'Barry.'
> 'Ha ha de ha ha ha, you didn't say no.'

This acme of intellectual subtlety has been translated for adults to be known as open questions. To put it simply, the words 'who', 'what', 'why', 'where', 'when', 'which' and 'how' inserted into questions will not allow the answer 'no', or so the theory goes. Although I delight in taking the micky out of the theorists who stick rigidly to this, I also agree that questions are the most powerful tools in the seller's cellar.

The Approach

> 'Can I help you?'
> 'No, just looking.'

This is called the approach. If you are going to open a business where the customer comes to you, be it boat marina, shop, garden centre or junk yard, how are you going to approach your customers? More to the point, why are you going to approach your customers?

In our example case, the dollop would say 'To see if they need any help.' The reason I offer to you is that you approach them with a view to selling them something and you ask questions to gain information to help with this. A rather vicious game you can play to illustrate the futility of current practice is to go into a shop and wait to be asked 'Can I help you?' You reply 'With what?' and then remain silent while this little grenade does its devastating work. It isn't long before panic sets in and our victim rushes off howling. Perhaps this is why my family refuses to go into shops with me. What has gone wrong? Is it the 'no' answer?

What Do You Do with Them if You Catch Them?

The shops and offices have all leapt eagerly on this open-question bandwagon and have cheerfully put a nice open 'how' in front of the stock phrase. So now we get 'How can I help you?' or supposedly even better 'How may I help you?' This grates on me and I believe still doesn't get anywhere.

There is a joke which kind of illustrates the problem. A woman is talking to her neighbour:

'I'm sorry to tell you this, but I saw your husband chasing a pretty young woman in the pub yesterday.'
'Was he really? Can't say I'm bothered.'
'You're not?'
'Nah, we once had a dog that used to chase cars, but if he had ever caught one, he wouldn't have been capable of driving it.'

The staff have been shown in a crude sort of way how to chase the customers, but they wouldn't know what to do if they caught one.

Now prepare yourself, because when you approach your customers, I am going to suggest something pretty radical. How about 'Hello' as an opening, or even 'Good morning' or 'Good afternoon'? After all, what you need to do is to make contact in the nicest possible way. If you have got the nerve after the initial hello, you remain silent. The customer tends to then involve you in conversation: 'Er oh hello, um are these the only colours you have?'

The Hedgehog

There is a jolly old sales trick known as the 'hedgehog close'. This suggests that a customer who throws you questions is in fact throwing you a prickly hedgehog which makes you want to throw it straight back. Or, in other words, answer questions with a question. In actual fact it works rather well, as long as you don't lose control:

'What colour were you looking for?'
'Well, red would be nice.'

Now here you have an opportunity to get commitment from the customer. If you don't have red we must steer them elsewhere, but if you do, don't rush to admit it by saying something like 'Oh red's no problem, we've always got plenty of red ones.' That may seem helpful but it doesn't turn the customer's screw. Try 'Red, oh I'm not sure if I have got any left. Let me go and see. How many did you want?' 'Oh, just the one.' Can you see what has happened? They have bought it.

Perhaps you have got a stock room full of them, but then a good poker player doesn't play with his cards face up. In fact, what we advise is to go off for a while, then come back with cobwebs in your hair, a flesh wound in your arm, a distinct limp and carrying two of them in red. 'I managed to find two.' It isn't guaranteed, but the customer often takes both.

Play Hard to Get

The same principle can be applied to those big-sale folk who have moved heaven and earth to get that once-in-a-lifetime appointment. For example, Mr buyer says 'Of course, we have to have fish on Fridays.' You leap forward to the edge of your chair with an eager but open smile. 'That's no problem, we can easily do that.' The great poker player doesn't break into an eager but open smile and say 'Yes, yes, I've got four aces,' well not until after he has seen the colour of your money.

'Mmm Fridays, mmm fish, tell me, is that very important to you?' 'Of course, the contract hinges on it.' Think for a while, do some complicated calculations on the calculator, write something, purse your lips and reluctantly say as if soundly beaten by his perspicacity, 'So, if we undertake to provide fish on Friday, you will grant us this contract?' To sum up this little detour, when we approach customers, we only ask questions that give us the information that will help us to sell them something.

Why? Why? Why?

Now we'll look at the very considerable power of open questions for good and bad. There is no doubt that they are great persuaders, but just like a hand grenade, their power can blow your hand off if you don't chuck them in the right direction.

An example is the use of the word 'why'. On the face of it, you would think it is the ideal word for finding reasons for actions as in 'Why did you do that?' The problem is that whatever our customer has done or is going to do, it is the result of their decision-making process. If you call that process into question, you are, in a roundabout way, attacking their judgement. People are fragile, sensitive little creatures and if you challenge their judgement, they frantically start to justify their actions until they completely believe their own old baloney. At this point, their commitment is unshakeable and we are lost.

Al Capone classically said when given a bit of a talking to about beating people to death with baseball bats and racketeering, 'Why do you attack me when all I tried to do was give people a bit of innocent fun?' The scary thing is that he believed it. You must avoid provoking the customer into justifying their actions or they will convince themselves beyond your ability to get them back. For instance:

'Thank you for your time, but I am not sure at this time if we are ready to change to your company.'
'Oh, why is that?' [Now you've done it, watch the justification start.]
'Well, for a start, we are very happy with our current supplier. I don't think you have put forward a convincing case and, to be frank, your product's disappointing.'

Now, try putting that right. Lets rerun that:

'Thank you for your time, but I am not sure at this time if we are ready to change to your company.'

'Oh, I am sorry to hear that. We were really looking forward to working with you. Look, what do we have to do to secure your business?'

Can you see how that might work better than that challenging 'why?'.

By the way, to sling in a touch of sophistication here, a skilled professional negotiator would have noticed the customer said 'not sure at this time'. This is apparently a signal, as opposed to 'Sod off, I wouldn't do business with you if my life depended on it,' which I suppose is also a signal but probably one that suggests you should get on your bike. The previous one, however, shows a chink of light. A ray of hope. Others like that would be 'not at those prices', 'I can't see this working with your current attitude'. Although they sound negative, they are signals that show a willingness to deal, and beg for questions like 'So which prices would you deal at?' or 'Tell me what attitude you think is appropriate and we will make every effort to fit in,' followed by 'If you can guarantee us this contract.'

Any road up, we were dealing with 'why'. Because of its provocative nature, the gurus will suggest you avoid it, but what it provokes is justification and there is nothing wrong with positive justification. You just need the courage to provoke it. 'Look, we are thinking of changing and using your company.' Most people would start leaping round the office whooping and yelling 'Oh yes! Come to me big boy. Have you made the right decision. You won't regret it, we won't let you down,' to which you get, 'Listen, I said thinking,' as the customer back-pedals, scared by your outburst. Try, 'That's great. Why did you choose us?' which can provoke 'Well we heard you were reliable, I like your prices, and our current supplier has become just a bit too relaxed.' 'That's wonderful, when would you like us to start?' The justification is in your favour.

POINTS TO PONDER

1 Don't show and tell. You're there to sell. You've got in front of your client, now for Pete's sake, understand what you are there for.

2 Develop that checklist and stick to it. Don't lose sight of the goal.

3 If you know your product is inferior, don't bother calling until it isn't.

4 Develop the gift of the earhole, not the gift of the gab.

5 Don't be afraid to measure your progress. After all, you need to know where you are to be sure of where you are going.

6 Understand the difference between a major sale and a minor sale. If it is a major sale, take it one step at a time.

7 Consider the consequences of a customer changing their business to you, an unknown and unproven quantity. Success will lie in the proof.

8 Just because your target customer's current supplier is totally awful, it doesn't mean that they will change from them.

9 Going on forever with no measurable result is a failure: a long, slow dreary failure.

10 Don't get ambushed. Be gently assertive about some where to conduct your sale, and if all else fails, the best you can get is a firm appointment where the omens and environment are more conducive to your success.

11 Don't accept a drink.

12 Know why you approach customers and what you will do with them when you catch them.

13 Don't ask 'why'. It causes negative justification. Ask 'how' and look for signals.

9

Questions, Questions, Questions

The main reason for asking questions is to gain information, and I would describe the initial part of my sale as the investigation phase. This is where I find out as much as possible about the client: what they need, what their current position is, and how to avoid mistakes through misunderstanding.

This is a very tricky area. For a long time it was accepted that questions were asked to identify a need. Your products were aligned to satisfy that need, and a sale was made. The truth is that very few people see themselves as having any sort of burning need (well not to buy anything at any rate). What most people do accept, however, is that they have problems. Most products or services are bought to solve problems. 'I am too fat': buy a slimming product; 'I want to be admired': buy a sports car (sad, I know); 'We make the stuff, but I can't get it delivered': hire a haulage firm.

Our problem is that what we make or do is designed to satisfy a need, so when we meet the customer, it is like trying to put a three-pin plug into a two-pin socket – we need an adapter. The danger lies in misinterpreting the customer's stated problem as a need. Here is an example:

'My window cleaner has let me down again.'
'That's no problem, we can do you right away.'
'Mmm, perhaps I'll let you know.' = FAILURE

'I can't get these accounts to add up.'
'With our computer you could.'
'Not at your prices I couldn't.' = FAILURE

THE ADAPTER

You see that as the customer states the problem, we think we hear a need, when all the customer did was imply a need. So we fit in an adapter, convert that problem to a real need for what we are selling.

'My window cleaner has let me down again.'

First Step: Sympathize and Question

'Oh no, poor old you, he hasn't? What a shame. Has that happened before?
'Yes.'

Second Step: Discuss the Implications

'It is so depressing when the house is all gloomy because the windows are dirty, and I suppose in a way it can reduce the value of your house when the windows don't look clean, can't it?'
'I hadn't looked at it like that.'

Third Step: The Solution

'Look, wouldn't you say that what you need is a reliable service that you can depend on without having to worry every week?'

BINGO! We have converted the problem to a need. Obviously, a sincere business conversation would be more subtle than this, but I am sure you have got the idea. Did you notice that it was all expressed as questions?

REMEMBER, QUESTIONS PERSUADE

They also inform. We have a disastrous habit of jumping to conclusions. If a customer tells you 'I want the finest one you can make,' the little gears and wheels in our head start spinning out of control. We think 'The finest? I could use pure platinum for the trim, and if the spindles were diamond encrusted I could use gold on the counterbalance.' The customer snaps us from our reverie by asking 'What sort of money are we talking?' 'Oh I don't know, I could do something quite special for about 50 grand.' With this our customer runs off screaming.

The point is that we know our business, its jargon and prices so well that we often forget that our customers don't. Because of that we misunderstand what they want. Just to remind you, the bit of our checklist we are working on is the 'What have I learned ... ' bit. Just so that there can be no mistake, I like to call that bit 'investigation'.

INVESTIGATION

Just like a great detective, you are going to use careful questioning to assemble all the clues to what the customer *really* wants. It is no good rushing about the place accusing the butler of whacking Lord Snotty over the head with a lead pipe in the library if you have got no facts to support it. Let's try it. Take your notebook and pen – no I'm not joking, writing things down has a threefold good effect:

1 It stops you forgetting key facts.
2 It looks very professional.
3 It allows you to control the pace of the interview.

'Could you hold on a moment while I make a note of that?'
'I want the finest one you can make.'

'Great, is it for a special occasion?' (questions and hedgehogs)
'Yep, my son's wedding, no expense spared.'
'Wonderful. Have you bought one before?'
'Yes, we had a fine one for my daughter's wedding.'
'Where did you get that one from?'
'Woolworths I think.'
'Were you happy with that one?'
'I thought it was a bit expensive for what it was, but then, you don't stint on your kids do you?'
'No, that's right, so do you have a price in mind?'

JOURNEY INTO THE PAST

Before we go on, you will notice that the customer was questioned about the past as in 'Have you bought one before?' There is a great psychological reason for this. If you just leap out at people, fix them with your best gimlet stare, and then ask them their future buying plans, they will tend to get a bit tetchy, because you are prying into their present and future affairs. The past, however, doesn't offer quite the same threat, and people are much more relaxed talking about it. When rapport is established, it doesn't take much to swing the past to the future: 'Have you bought one before? Would you buy another?'

I know we are trying to build the big picture here and take you through the minefield of how to win those major clients, but this exercise alone can build into a fine little sales technique all on its own. Remember, you have been pacing the interview by asking questions, listening and writing things down. There is a point where things go sort of quiet, embarrassingly quiet in fact. No, stay cool, don't break down and start blabbering on as the pressure of silence builds. Let a wistfully knowing smile play fleetingly across your reassuringly professional lips as your eyes darken into bottomless wells of trustworthy knowledge. A slight flicker of your fine-scribed eyebrows should be enough to provoke, 'So, where do I go from here?' from the customer.

This will be a cue to translate your notes for them, and to remind them of all the good things that are in store. Unless you are a complete prat, you will resist reminding them of the bad things that they felt were also waiting. Getting a good relaxed eye contact with the customer, using your tasteful but fine quality pen as a pointer to guide you, you review the notes.

'Now, you said that your current one was wearing out,' pause, more pause, a tiny bit more pause. 'Yes?'

'Oh, er, yes.'

'Mmm,' a gentle tick with that pen.

'Although you mentioned that money was tight, it was essential to have a reliable one,' less of a pause. 'Yes?'

'Yes.'

'Now you also said that if it could be delivered on site, it would save a fortune,' no pause 'yes? And your favourite colour was red.'

'Yes.'

'OK, then let me suggest the following plan of action. If you can give me the go-ahead today, I will supply a brand-new one in red to your site with a 24-month guarantee. And, to set your mind at rest about the cost problem, I will defer payment for 12 months and then organize a lease at less than £200 per month. Isn't that less than 10 per cent of what it will be earning?'

'Yes.'

Facetious and oily, it may be, but it is also confident and well controlled. Summaries can get you that control of the interview, and don't worry: oiliness takes years to acquire and we will burn that bridge when we come to it. It is clear, then, that questions give us information and information is power.

QUESTIONS GIVE US POWER

Questions also give us status, which is something we desperately need. You will notice that I have been banging on about the gift of the earhole, or in other words, 'shut up and sell', and so does every sales training course and book. There are two reasons. One is because asking questions and listening is very effective. Two is because a poor little tatty sales representative feels completely at the bottom of the heap, and the professional buyer is often trained in the skills of seller humiliation, and delights in using those skills. Our poor little rep knows he should keep his gob shut, but bowel control is already under threat as soon as he sets foot in the terror's office, and as with most salesmen, bowels and mouth seem to be inextricably linked. Trouble is brewing.

'Well thank you for seeing me, Mr Thumbscrew.' Ploy number one: fix salesman with cockatrice stare, continue with an icy silence. No more ploys are required and a total loss of control over both key orifices is achieved. 'Well, Mr Thumbscrew, the reason I called was ... gabble, gabble, gabble.' One hour later: 'gabble ... what do you think Mr Thumbscrew?' More stares, more silence, but now with a slow, sneery smile. 'There's nothing new there. You have wasted my time, Mr Sadgit. Next time don't bother unless you really have something to show me.' Our hero leaves beaten and humiliated.

This is a fate we have to avoid at all costs. Many of you who are tempted to Go It Alone have quite high levels of professional skills which, quite rightly, you have decided to market to make your own crust. Perhaps in the guise of a consultant. Just consider the implications of the fact that you will be your own salesperson, and if you crawl away from the client, flatulent and humiliated, it doesn't exactly inspire them to put the reorganization of their business empire in your hands or, for that matter, the servicing of their treasured car, the celebration meal for their 50th anniversary or the treatment of their dog. We must have status for the sake of credibility.

For some reason that I don't entirely understand, people who ask more questions have more status. Just test the theory yourself. When a lowly, contemptible creature last served you in a shop, did it ask questions? When you got stopped for speeding and you sat and quaked, I bet you were asked loads of questions. 'Did you know how fast you were going? Didn't you notice the school? Do you have your documents?' I bet your mind wasn't wandering at that barrage. People who ask questions get attention. People who have attention have status. Status with another valuable extra, and that is control. What I offer you in your new business interviews is status with control.

Before

'What's this going to cost me?'

'Er, look um, we would sort of be talking around, um, a thousand.'

'Ridiculous.'

'Of course, that isn't fixed, we could probably find a, you know ...'

After

'What's this going to cost me?'

You, with confident eye contact: 'Before we deal with the price, Mr Smith, may I ask you a question?' Silence. A bit more silence, then:

'Er yes, please do.'

'You say that your current one is leaking. How much fluid are you having to buy?'

Putty in your hands. Think doctor, think judge, think about any cool, collected, confident professional that asks questions from a position of status, and you are on your way.

The thing that triggered all this off was question two on our checklist (*see Chapter 8*), which was: 'What information have I gathered that will be of use to me in future dealings with this client?' Now you have learned how to ask questions, you can now gather that useful information:

'So you are retiring, Mr Smith, tell me, who's taking over your position?'

'You have met him, my assistant Martin.'

'Oh I am pleased to hear that. I will congratulate him (grovel and crawly bum lick if necessary) on my way out. So who deals with this for the fourth floor?,' or 'When does the board meet to discuss this?'

By now, you must be getting the idea that the art of persuasion lies in asking questions. As we wend our merry way to the conclusion of our presentation bit, you will see that whatever activity takes place in this line will always benefit from the use of questions.

The third item on the checklist will require considerably less time spent on it than the previous ones, simply because it is very similar. It is:

3 WHAT INFORMATION HAVE I GATHERED THAT WILL BE OF USE TO ME WITH FINDING AND KEEPING OTHER CLIENTS?

In other words, you use this gained 'intelligence' to help find new customers with questions like:

'So, who's building that factory next door?'

'Punka, I think.'

'Punka? I've not come across them.'

'Yes, you know them, it's all the old trinket people. Mike Jackson's heading them up. You must remember him.'

This also gives you a hook when later you ring Mike Jackson:

'Mr Jackson? Oh, nice to speak to you. I was with Bill Bumper, yes that's right, Bill Bumper, and we were admiring your new plant. It is certainly taking shape, and that's why I was ringing because ...'

Do you get the idea? When you go out to promote yourself and your enterprise, don't give information out; be prepared to sponge it up. When you buy a profitable going concern for some astronomical sum, one of the things you pay for is the so-called goodwill. Goodwill, on one hand, may be the loyalty of the current customers, but it is also years of knowledge and market intelligence. By using the former methods, you can acquire the requisite knowledge at a quite alarming pace (well, alarming to your competitors at any rate) without having to resort to buying it.

My final call on the checklist is:

4 IF I DID THIS ONE AGAIN, WHAT WOULD I HAVE DONE BETTER?

Even if the thing was the biggest success ever, and you have come away with a cheque for £50,000, you still can find room for improvement. If you watch any premier sporting team after a game, they will analyse their play and look for improvement, even if they won convincingly. This means that at every step you will be getting better. Even if your competitors look at you with envy, by the time they have caught up to where you were, you will now, by continuous improvement, be somewhere better and impossible to catch.

A HORRIBLE END

The part where most people go horribly wrong is near the end, where they fail to clinch the deal. This is one of the essentials, and we must look at it.

One of the difficulties is realizing and reading the apparent character changes the buyer goes through just before making their decision. In classic sales parlance, what happens once you have got the customer interested is that one supposedly makes a 'trial close'. This is a confection of linguistic finesse, with a web of subtle nuance garnished with penetrating insight. As I can't be bothered with all that old tosh, for the sake of example we will use: 'Well, mush, are you going to buy it then?' Perhaps a little thin on subtlety, but it will produce an effect: 'No.'

Actually, 'no' is surprisingly quite rare; it is more often a frustratingly woolly, 'Well, I might, but I need to think about it.' If we accept that as kind of negative, we need to ask ourselves why the client is negative. Now it is the belief of our oily chums that the customer has an objection to the proposition, which may be spoken: 'No, it is too dear,' or unspoken, 'Ummmmmmm,' to which we fire in questions to uncover the unspoken objection. Once the objection is securely understood, received wisdom will have us believe that the objection can be dealt with. Again, this is really a major sales technique, but some grasp of it will not go amiss.

Before we start on that, however, I would just like you to consider a great worry of mine. I don't know how to put this question politely, so I won't, and here goes: ARE YOU CRAP?

You see, this selling-yourself lark shouldn't be as difficult as most salespeople would have you believe. If you follow the simple rules in the preceding chapter, and come across as a subtle, well-controlled professional, the customer should judge your offer on its merits. If, from your presentation, they judge what you offer as the best they have seen, at good value, they must buy. 'But,' I hear them wail, 'I am not the best, and on value it's awful.' If that is the case you have got to be the best salesperson ever, and should be prepared to emigrate as soon as you get your hands on the cash.

I must have a heart-to-heart with you about my own business. Major manufacturing companies come and ask me what is wrong with their salesforce because their market share is dropping. When I meet the salesforce, there seems very little wrong with them except a bit of demoralization, but when I see the product, there is plenty wrong. It is overpriced, it is old fashioned, it is unreliable, and the rest of the company is completely unable to give good service. The competition provides well-priced, completely reliable, cutting-edge technology, and the whole company is dedicated to excellent service. My moral dilemma is, do I plod on with the sales-training pretence, or tell my client that it is all over for them? If you don't think people could be that stupid, look at the history of the motor industry.

IF WHAT YOU OFFER IS THE BEST AVAILABLE IN THE WHOLE WORLD, IT IS MUCH EASIER TO SELL!

So, ask yourself every day, 'Am I the best in the whole world?' If the answer is 'No, Julia Higgins is better,' ask yourself why, and pinch her ideas.

Some people, because they are small, think that it is a fine art to be crap. We had a decorator in whose enthusiastic incompetence earned him the soubriquet 'Mr Splashy'. His argument against my splattered furniture, carpets and windows was that he was 'cheaper than them town 'uns'. Being a 'one-person band' is an opportunity for excellence, not to be cheap. If you are brilliant at selling yourself, it is no good if people will only do business with you once, and if you are the best in the world and no one gets to hear of you, that is almost more tragic. You can't have one without the other. BEST IN THE WORLD OR DON'T BOTHER.

BEST IN THE WORLD? THEN TELL THE WORLD ABOUT IT

Despite all this, the sales superstars will still expect objections, and will have a bag of well-oiled routines to deal with them. Routines that, if tried by the beginner or the underconfident, are toe-curlingly awful. Having said all of that, there is quite a bit of value to be gained for us by having just a touch of the pro's courage.

Although I am loath to admit it, I suppose the unspoken objection does exist, and if we don't know about it, we can't handle it. We have been chatting away with our new contact, and seem to be getting on very nicely, but time is getting on and we would rather like that £50,000 catering contract. So now what do you do? It is time to leave and it would be nice to leave with something. The customer is giving us clues that we are starting to outstay our welcome: maybe he is filling a hot water bottle, or perhaps he is slumbering gently:

'Well, thank you so much for your time, Mr Conker. Can I ask you if I am likely to be considered for the catering contract?'

Not a great ending, but we will have another go at that in a moment. For now it is the answer we are interested in: 'We will have to see. My office will contact you if we wish to take things further.' NO. That is not 'v. int', it is 'v. not int'. It is just another way of saying don't call us, we'll call you.

Let's just think about this. We know the job is up for grabs, and it is starting to look as though we are not going to get it. We need to know why, and the only person who knows is the buyer. OK, so gather every atom of courage and ask him. Even if it enrages him into calling security to have you flung in the street (which it won't), nothing is lost if you weren't going to get the job anyway. The way you ask could smooth things along. It is not a good idea, for example, to lift him out of his chair by the lapels, press your nose to his and yell 'You Liar! You have no intention of doing business with me. Now tell me why not before I break every bone in your body.' This could easily provoke the being-flung-in-the-street option, and I would recommend as a slightly less controversial alternative: 'You don't seem too sure, Mr Conker. What is it that I have not explained that has failed to convince you?' Then shut up. There is a good chance he will tell you what his objection is.

Now forget all the slimy stuff and just stick to a simply honest and upfront investigation of the problem by asking questions. 'Not experienced enough, you say? Would you help me a lot by just clarifying that?' Notice the walking-on-eggshells questions when the temptation is to say 'Experienced? I spend my whole life doing this and you have the brass neck to suggest I am not experienced. Well let me tell you pal ...' Can you hear the distant trap-trap of the security guards' hobnail boots? By being gentle and careful with our questions, we may not only get valuable answers, but we may also get the client to reassess his position.

When you have got the objection out, please don't contradict it, or it is street time again. Try: 'Now I can understand your being concerned that your new caterer should be experienced. It is a very important consideration. That is why these testimonials may set your mind at rest. I am sure you will agree that for

Consolidated International to give us such a glowing report, we must have been pretty good.' Now wait.

TOMORROW, THE WORLD

The secret for the Go-It-Aloner is really to have the bottle to ask those key questions, or to put it another way, it means you could target any potential customer in the whole world. Maybe the President of the USA himself. Give him a call and say:

'Watcha Prez, me old pal. How about letting me handle your security?' to which he may say:
'Well thank you for your time. I'll look at your proposal and ring you if we need anything.' But that is not what he is thinking. Theory states that if you have the courage to uncover that thinking, you are in with a chance.
'Come off it Prez, I can see you are not sure. Now what is bothering you? You can tell me.' 'Well the USA is kinda large, do you think you could manage it on your own?'
'Lord bless you Prez, you are a caution an' no mistake. Look, when I done the People's Republic of China job, I 'ad some very trustworthy lads to help. Would it help if you met them?'

The only reason anyone in the world doesn't buy from us is because they have an objection, or to express it better, a concern. If, by asking questions and giving gentle answers and explanations, we can handle those concerns, the business is ours.

The next bit involves all the elements of uncovering objections that we have just discussed, but it also concerns a paradox. That is that when potential customers are being friendly and co-operative with you, they are unlikely to buy, but when they become horrible and picky, they are more likely to buy. Before you start thinking that I have gone round the bend, consider your own buying decisions. Maybe you are half-thinking of buying a new television. You amble around the shop, admiring this and admiring that. The salesperson involves you in conversation about the features of the Yamabongy 65 RM Pro Logic, and you are wowed by its abilities. You smile at the salesperson, thank them profusely for their time, and go away to think about things.

The change comes when you have made up your mind to buy, and return to the store. The salesperson greets you like an old friend, but the smile fades from their face when they see your grim expression. You start to ask tough questions about price and reliability, and why you should buy it from their store. The reason you have done a Jekyll and Hyde on them is because now you have a genuine desire to buy and are going to start spending your hard-earned cash, things are getting serious.

HAPPY TO SEE YOU, NOT HAPPY TO BUY

Let's consider the attitude of a benign company director. He has got a quiet afternoon; he has played with all his executive toys and then you breeze in. He sits you down, perhaps has a coffee with you (remember the dangers of accepting coffee), and listens to your tale. He chuckles at your jokes and offers encouragement. What he sees is a beginner whom he feels sorry for. He won't hurt your feelings by saying anything he feels is unkind. What he knows is that he pays a fortune to hire some of the world's top professionals, to whom he gives a hard time because he needs results. At the end of listening patiently to your presentation, he smiles and shakes your hand warmly as he shows you out. He even secretly and genuinely wishes you success. You write 'v. int' and do a little victory dance in his car park.

Well I hate to yet again shatter the illusion, but he isn't the slightest bit 'v. int'. Let's play it again. He is listening patiently and you start to ask probing questions and offer solutions that, if true, would mean real benefit to him. His eyes narrow and he sits forward in his chair. 'Are you telling me I am stupid to deal with my current supplier, suppliers that I have been happy with for years?' What has happened? That great big pussy cat who was being so nice to us has now suddenly turned into a tiger, and I now tell you that this is a good sign. The reason is that when he had no intention to buy from you, he had no cause to get tough. Now your questions have provoked him into seriously considering your proposition, he will ask tough questions. Just don't lose your nerve, and answer calmly:

'Of course I am not suggesting that you are being stupid. In fact I am sure you deal with them very shrewdly, and that you have been successful to date by being very careful about whom you choose to supply you, but I am sure you will agree that times change, and even if you don't choose a completely new supplier, it is not a bad idea to have a good one as a second string to your bow, that can fill a percentage of the order to spread the risk as it were.'

'And you think you can be my second string. What proof do you have?'

I hope you do have some proof, or you could be up the creek. Actually, what you have here is a very interesting situation which raises some valuable points. First, why are we going to talk to this bloke about his £50,000 catering project?

WHERE'S THE PROOF?

It hardly seems likely that you will be handed a £50,000 contract without some kind of evidence of your ability to do the job. If you had a genuine intention to secure the job you would have brought the proof with you. This proof of ability can take all kinds of shapes. One can be the impression that you make – cheap, shoddy clothes, scabby business cards, naff brochures will all put you out of the running. You could have references or testimonials, or you could offer a demonstration of you or your product's talents.

This raises the next important point. You will notice that we have got to a very interesting and critical stage with our potential client. I would say that if substantial proof were offered and accepted, we are in with a fair shout. So, what of the eager beaver who is granted that once-in-a-lifetime interview, and prepares his demonstration (or 'dem' as it is known in photocopier parlance) and his brochures, only to explode through the customer's door like a sort of infernal cabaret. Remember the 'Well, what have you got to show me?' trap the customer lays for us. All of your bits and bobs are there for that crucial moment in the conversation when the customer wants evidence, so KEEP YOUR POWDER DRY until it is time to use it.

THEY WANT YOU, BUT DON'T WANT YOU TO KNOW

The next aspect of the customer becoming difficult is a bit more sinister. Again it is a ploy that probably isn't unknown to you, and one you may well have used when the boot was on the other foot, as it were. This concerns the customer who has completely made up their mind to buy from you. They have budgeted to your price, your quality and your terms. So, what the hell, if they can squeeze a bit more out of you, it is all a bonus.

It is a game worth playing so long as you understand it's a game. It is just a bit disconcerting if you didn't spot it. A minion may receive your quote and tell his boss, who then tells him the quote is fine and to stop wasting time and give you the job immediately. Of course you don't know this, and the sly buyer will feign disinterest and maybe he will 'give you a chance' for a bit more discount. The answer to this? Well, ain't life a bitch, because I don't know. I hate finding myself in that situation because you don't know if they are bluffing. All you can do is turn up the professionalism wick by pulling out a precise client file with copies of all quotes and conversations with this client, where you gently remind him how in previous negotiations his consummate skill had caused you to cut prices to the bone. You also need to know in your own mind which prices are realistic to you before you discount away your profit. Having said that, you will have to throw this dog some kind of a bone, in the shape of a minor concession which he can interpret as a victory, or you will have an enemy for life.

REMEMBER, KEEP YOUR HEAD. STAY PROFESSIONAL

The moment has come. This is nirvana for all salespeople. The close. This is the moment when the prospective customer is finally invited to buy. This is not a book on the finer nuances of sales technique, but can I remind you where we started in this section? For pity's sake, remember to ask people to buy something. It breaks my heart to see all you talented people so packed with ability and enthusiasm sink, just because you lacked the bottle or know-how just to ask.

Having said that, there are certain ways to ask and salespeople would have you believe that these are the closing techniques. Some even carry in their heads what they call their bag of closes. There is the puppy dog close, the right angle, the George Washington, the Duke of York and the arm lock, to name a few. Mostly old cobblers, and quite difficult to use if you want to avoid looking a prat. I can recommend a couple, however.

The Alternative asks you to give the customer two choices, both of which result in business for you. For instance, 'Well I think that's about everything. Would you want me to start right away, or is Monday soon enough?' 'Did you want the red or the green?' And so on. More subtle and professional is to use that list we have been making whilst in conversation with the customer. Run through those agreed points, and then propose action:

'Now you said the other people let you down?'
'Yes.'
'And you need it by next week?'
'Yes.'
'You like our colour and the prices as long as we give you 10 per cent discount for cash?'
'Yes.'
'Then may I suggest that you just OK the order, and we can get started?'

JOB DONE!

But not quite. Your whole future depends on your ability to get work, and despite my cheery and breezy description that precedes this point, be under no illusions: it can be tough, costly and time-consuming. Bearing that in mind, when you have got a customer, consider what, even in terms of mental torment, it has cost you to get them. Two points. One is: don't lose them, which is what we will be dealing with in the next section, and the other is: get the most out of them, or in other words, be prepared to sell them more.

In classic sales parlance there is a beasty called the 'add-on' or 'linked sale'. This seems to mean when you buy a pair of shoes, a huge balloon of a thing leaps out at you and shrieks, 'D'you want any polish?'

SELL 'EM MORE

The efficacy of this manoeuvre, whilst in some doubt, does have a point, and that is to maximize each sale. From our point of view, the whole thing is more relevant, and can be handled in a relaxed but profitable manner.

I am sure that you have unfailingly absorbed every word I have written, and your loins are well and truly girded for financial victory over the dragons of skintness, but I still say that initially the biggest trouble you are going to have is finding customers and lucrative work. With this in mind, make sure that you get the most out of each and every customer. Even if you are considering painting and decorating, and you have been asked to quote for painting the drawing room, offer a combined price for the hall, stairs and dining room. With a restaurant, always ask if they would like some pudding. If you flog atomic power stations, offer to do the decommissioning project. You might fear that this will put customers off, but it doesn't: it shows you care enough to anticipate their needs. They will love you, and best of all, it doesn't even leave a crumb for your competitor.

You may feel we have spent a lot of time on this selling bit, but in my experience it is what the 'Go-It-Aloner' stands or falls on. If you have the ability to find and keep customers, you are unlikely to lose. People try to challenge my view by offering evidence of the small business that went bust through over-trading, or by being snowed under by work. This plays into my hand because it is the strongest possible evidence of an inability to sell. Anyone can give stuff away and will probably generate a queue of people ready to take advantage of their stupidity. Over-traders go bust because the cost of borrowing exceeds their income. The prices you charge must pay all of your costs, hidden and otherwise, realize you a handsome enough profit to live the lifestyle you desire, have a surplus for eventualities and replacements, and give you a big enough stash to retire in some comfort. When you add all that together you will have a price, probably quite a high price.

To go over this again, when you look at your huge corporate competitors, their prices may seem high, and I despair when I see the aspiring 'Go-It-Aloner' gleefully telling me that they have an opportunity to undercut because of low overheads. Be warned: corporate players can borrow cheap, can buy cheap, can manufacture cheap, and they still lose money. If you want to fulfil the preceding wish-list, you can't be cheap; in fact, it may be worth considering being dear. I can buy high street shoes from a multiple store for £30, I will moan when a back-street cobbler charges me half their value at £15 to sole and heel them. It is the major part of the shoe and takes him hours, but I would be delighted to have a pair of shoes made by my personal boot-maker, and at the time of writing, the price in London for this is now £1,500.

Hang on! Before you rush out and multiply your prices by a factor of 20, you must realize the downside of this cunning strategy, and that is if you charge the highest prices in the world, you must be the best in the world, and the world has to know that. This means you must have the ability to thrill and delight every customer, and take it on the chin when you don't. We will deal with this in the next chapter.

For now, don't forget:

- Ask them to buy.
- Get that decision.
- And then sell them more.
- Your life depends on it.

POINTS TO PONDER

1 People don't feel they need to buy anything. We have to build this need by solving problems.
2 Investigate using questions to avoid confusion, and don't be afraid to write down the key facts.
3 Talk about the past; it puts people at ease.
4 Remind them of the good things they want, then suggest a plan of action.
5 Good questioning skills will give you the status you need to be convincing and the control you need for success.
6 Acquire market intelligence. For the new Go-It-Aloner, it is almost as good as buying a going concern with 'goodwill'.
7 You can always do better. If you are the best, it does make the whole thing easier.
8 Don't be brushed off. Uncover those hidden uncertainties.
9 These abilities mean that you can take on any customer in the whole world.
10 Difficult, picky people often buy, so make happy, friendly people difficult and picky, and the world's your oyster – maybe!
11 If you are going in to win the work, make sure you have brought irrefutable proof that you can do the job.
12 Sell yourself, sell your price, and then sell more.

10

Customers – Who Needs Them?

I am about to deal with the cringe-making subject of 'customer care'. Does this conflict with the initial and core values of this book? Now I have convinced you that the water is lovely, and have persuaded you to leap fully clothed into the limpid pool that is the life of a business rebel, I turn round and suggest behaving in an acceptable business manner.

Let's just look at our initial role model: the jungle freedom fighter. His, or her, success depends on travelling light, the correct use of modern weapons, and the element of surprise. The enemy, which is a large national army, fails because of its inability to respond quickly and its clumsy stupidity. Be reassured that it will not compromise your position if you use the modern weapons of close customer relationships, or fine precision marketing.

In my experience, the large companies, although they crow about it, have an attitude to customers that could be generously described as crap. So, when the service you give is truly exceptional, you will also be provided with that essential element of surprise. The customers will be surprised and delighted. Hold that sentence in your head as we start this little journey together.

THE MUGGER'S TALE

When I had a proper day job many years ago, I was struggling to decide what I could Go-It-Alone as. At the time there were some high-profile people making big bucks with huge, well-attended seminars on the subject of sales and how to get them. They went under the loose collective title of sales trainers, and eyeing their Rolls Royces and other extravagant accoutrements, I decided to become a sales trainer myself. It is relatively easy to show people how to sell things, and back then work was relatively easy to find. The problem arose from the objective the clients gave me. They would ring up and ask me to provide a bit of sales training for their 'team'. When I asked them what they wanted to achieve, they replied:

'To sell more.'
'So,' I would ask, 'You want them to sell more?'
'Yes, more,' they would chorus.
'More. Is that all?'
'More is all we want.'

This may seem a simple agenda, but it is its simplicity that is its downfall.

Say I asked you what secret you would like me to impart. Perhaps you would say:

'More money, show me how to get more money.'
'Is that all you want, more money?'
'Yes! More money.'

If that was your desire, then the best person to instruct you would be a mugger. He would show you which alleys to lurk in, what weapon to carry, and so on. As soon as you put his advice into practice, minutes after his instruction, you would have money. The only drawback being that a few short moments later you would be arrested.

Now it so happens that a great number of companies miss the ramifications of the arresting bit, and tend to use muggers to train their salesforce, blithely unaware of the consequences. If you feel that I exaggerate, you must ask yourself: who trained that person in the last car showroom you went into? That thing that came creeping up behind you, wringing its hands in greedy anticipation of lunching upon your liver and lights: 'Oh, 'ello, I see you're admiring the Thunderbolt 5000.'

The big bosses can't see the problem. Since they started mugging their customers, they can see that sales have shot up to a more than satisfactory level. Now they can forget about it and move on to the next thing on the agenda, which seems to be a disturbing rise in staff arrests and customer complaints. The training department are sent off to discover the root of the problem (nothing to do with mugging, you understand), and they come back with what they think is the solution:

'Well,' asks the El Supremo, 'Have you got a solution?'
'We have, your mightiness,' they whine in unison, 'It's the words, you see. When normal people do business with each other, they say things ...'
'What things? Have you made a note of these things?'
'We have, your greatness.'
'Well teach our team these "things" to say.'

Which they do, and they give the programme the spine-tingling title of 'customer care'. This raises the horrible spectre of a mugger that leaps out, holds a knife to your throat and says 'I'm Brian, your mugger for this evening! Thank you for sharing your wallet with me. Have a nice day. Missing you already.' Somehow it doesn't make us feel any better about being mugged.

The point is that we can't 'do' customer care; we have to 'care' about our customers. For a very valid reason, and that is that they earn us our money. Remember the often repeated saying: 'Finding and keeping customers is the only activity that generates income. All other activities involve us in cost.' Together we have just passed through the mugging, or more politely, the 'finding' stage. Make no mistake, a vital stage, the success of your whole project depends on 'finding customers', but now you have found them, let's think about keeping them.

LOSE FEWER CUSTOMERS, GET MORE MONEY

An astonishing statistic I heard the other day is that manufacturing industries lose around 25 per cent of their customer base each year. Of course, some of this can be put down to plague and pestilence, but a lot of the customers in that figure are stomping off because they have been annoyed or, in some ways worse, have drifted away because they have been forgotten and neglected. Apparently, if this figure could be reduced from 25 per cent to 20 per cent, it would add a full 100 per cent to the profit line.

Once again, I would like to draw your attention to the fact that this is a survival guide. How you can survive out there on your own without a whiff of social security or being forced ignominiously back to drudgery and dead-end employment? With that in mind, you must accept that a doubling of the profit could make all the difference and is therefore worth going for. Now it is also a fact that finding new customers could cost us around 14 times as much as keeping old ones. Again, the facts make the choices obvious. So why when I rang my bank to complain about some unforeseen charges did I get:

> 'Thank you for ringing International Bank, I'm Janeece, how may I help you?'
> 'Yes, why did 80 quid disappear from my account?'
> 'You will notice that you became overdrawn last month.'
> 'Yes, by 10p.'
> 'The amount is irrelevant. The fact is that you created a delinquent overdraft situation, and we were forced to charge punitive arrangement fees. If you don't like it, you can swivel on this.'

Of course, no one tells their faithful but intrinsically stupid computer that I am spitting feathers, and the next day it puts the lid on the situation by sending a letter that starts, 'Dear valued customer'. Meanwhile, the equally stupid computer from the bank next door has written to me to offer a free holiday in the Seychelles if I move my account to them. What did that just cost everybody? Your survival depends on you hanging on to your customers. I don't know how hard you think you need to work at that, but just consider how hard you are prepared to work to get new customers.

I don't know how far you have got with your enterprise while reading this book. You might be an old hand looking for fresh ideas, but maybe you haven't started yet. If that is the case, the most exciting time is about to come: getting ready for those first customers. All the time and trouble, the dreams, the polishing up of the act, all going towards that big day. If I now put on my dismal hat, I could say it's all downhill from now on.

WINNING A CUSTOMER IS JUST THE START OF LOSING THEM

When I worked in advertising, we would hear from time to time that a major company had shown some sign of dissatisfaction with its current agency. The trade paper would have the gossip that held the clues: 'Mega Bean Corporation to invite pitches. Corporate Marketing Director, Cyril Fig, denied that this was an indication that Mega Bean was shopping for a new agency.' We would be in there like a rat up a drainpipe.

The target company's directors would come down to the private box at the Monaco Grand Prix, they would be helicoptered to the Grand National, or maybe a bit of skiing at Aspen. But, and this is a monster but, there was a saying that warned: 'From the day we win the business, it is the start of the process that will lose the business.' In other words, if that massive wooing operation paid off and we secured the business, it was accepted that it was only a matter of time before we lost it. Maybe the customer would get invited to Monaco again, but they would never be the centre of attention like the latest targets were. Meanwhile, of course, as our client, they would have become our competitors' target for lavish entertainment. Unless you have limitless funds, when you have invested hard-earned cash and irreplaceable time on winning that customer, then you must keep them for ever.

KEEP THEM FOR EVER

One definition of this is 'repeat business', but how can we guarantee repeat business? The first inkling of trouble came about when Tom Peters suggested that customer satisfaction was no guarantee of repeat business. Well that set the cat among the pigeons, and no mistake. This is more vital to us than to anyone else because an established company with a large turnover only has to ensure that its sales and marketing department can win 25 per cent of new business, and it maintains the status quo. In our case, however, we are trying to build a business year on year, and cannot afford to lose one single customer.

Before Tom Peters' bombshell, every industry in the world would have said customer satisfaction is vital, but how do you judge it? The obvious answer was to ask the customer, but how? The solution appeared to be a thing called the CSI or Customer Satisfaction Index. The satisfaction could be crunched into manageable and measurable numbers by giving the customer questions that were within a tight format. Because of the basically tricky nature of the untrustworthy beast that is the customer, tick-box, multiple-questions forms are used. After all, we want their CSI, not their opinion, or so accepted practice will have us believe.

IBM are a case in point, I suppose, because they are a computer firm, and it stands to reason that it would be nice if their customers' responses could be converted into processable data. From this premise come tick-box forms that are classics of their type. For us, though, there is a big problem. Maybe we should instigate a CSI for our window cleaning round, maybe we should draw 50 grand from our savings and give it to an attitude research company to ascertain our CSI. Their researcher would leap out on our unsuspecting customers with a clipboard to ask those telling questions:

'Skews me, do you use the XL Window Company, and would you mind answering a few simple questions?'
'I suppose not.'

'Thank yew so much. Would you describe the performance of XL as satisfactory or not satisfactory?'

'Well, satisfactory.'

'Would you describe the behaviour of their operative on your premises as satisfactory or not satisfactory?'

'Satisfactory.'

'Would you describe their literature and paperwork as satisfactory or not satisfactory?'

'Satisfactory.'

This goes on for ages, but I am sure you get the idea. When you receive the results, you will be pleased to learn that you have achieved a score of no less than 94.6 per cent on the CSI. Surely this must mean our future is secure, but just think for a moment and ask yourself this: when was the last time you rushed up excitedly to one of your chums and said, 'Hey, you must go to that new restaurant in town. We went there the other night and, let me tell you, it was satisfactory'?

GOOD ENOUGH ISN'T

Now we can see why satisfaction just isn't enough. There was a lot of trouble a few years ago concerning the standards of workmanship when it came to manufacturing components. If you made cars, then you may well have invited someone to make exhaust systems. On your production line, your workers could have been paid for each car passing through. In any event, time was the master when it came to profit or loss. Therefore it would be very frustrating if these exhausts didn't fit. Maybe one would be a centimetre too long, another a few degrees more bent. With this problem to solve, it stood to reason that consistency was the key. To this end, a new discipline developed which was that of standards. In the UK there was a British standard number: BS 5750; the world took up ISO 9000. It meant that manufacturers would create an environment through manuals, measurement and management where consistency was inevitable.

A very useful programme. But then, in my humble opinion, things started to go wrong. The big manufacturers (probably quite rightly) started to insist that their suppliers should be certificated to BS 5750 or ISO 9000. The thing flipped over, and it was understood that if a small supplier achieved the certification, it would get some clout. A telling conversation took place when I was talking to a group of small companies about achieving these certifications. I asked, 'If you could buy these certificates off a guy in a bar, how many of you would be here today?' There was not a forest of hands.

QUALITY: I KNOW IT WHEN I SEE IT

The next problem arose when this all started getting tangled up with quality. I have always maintained it is only about consistency, which can be a good thing of course, but people started to drift into calling it quality. Those exhaust pipes still rust out within two years; in fact they all rust out in 22 months, 1 week, 2 days, 4 hours and 3 minutes – that is consistency, not quality. Now because you can manage consistent production, if you can transpose consistent with quality, this bizarre alchemy allows you theoretically to manage quality. This new arcane art has earned the title of TQM, or Total Quality Management. I would go along with total consistency management, but quality?

If a company makes meat pies and I don't like them, then in my eyes they are bad meat pies. If they are always the same, then they are consistently bad meat pies. You will say to me, 'Who is to say what is a bad meat pie?' and I will cheerfully reply 'ME,' and you will say 'You've got a cheek. Who gave you the right to condemn their pies?' 'I did.' As a customer like you, or any other customer, I have every right to say what I think is bad. If your customers describe what you do or make as bad, you are lost, no matter what code numbers you apply. People who defend this say that it means that products can be made up to a certain standard. Condemned out of their own mouths! UP TO a certain standard. But not beyond.

One of the seminal hippy handbooks is *Zen and the Art of Motorcycle Maintenance*. It is a rambling, navel-examining book which is most difficult to read, but I recommend that you try, if only for the bit on quality and how individuals perceive it. Of course, if your enterprise will benefit from achieving the standard codes of BS 5750 or ISO 9000, then go for it, but they will only make you satisfactory. To get these premium fees that I want for you, we are going to have to be a lot better than satisfactory. Worse than that, the only person qualified to judge whether you are achieving those heady heights are your customers.

What if we hire our expensive survey people once again for our window cleaning business, but this time we change the questions?

CHANGE THE QUESTIONS

What if our questioner asked:

'When XL come to clean your windows, do you become uncontrollably excited?'
'No.'
'When they have finished, do you chuckle with happiness?'
'No.'
'Are you thrilled?'
'No.'
'Does it make you happy?'
'No.'

Now you have scored a CSI of zero. I am sure you have started to see where I am coming from, and so have a lot of other people. Big industry has realized that it is relatively easy to install the BS 5750 and the ISO 9000, and even to pay lip service to this thing they call TQM, but then their competitors have all done the same. So how do you get ahead of the competition?

They then read the gobbledygook that business gurus like me churn out, and they look into this customer bit. Their rocky road started with the premise, 'Anyone can satisfy their customers; to get the edge we must DELIGHT ours.' The next day, every staff-training module was changed from 'Personal Hygiene for Saturday Staff', to 'Delighting the Customer'. Some even made the horrible cringe-making mistake of writing it all over their vans and literature: 'We want you to be DELIGHTED'. It is like a drowning man clinging to a happy, buoyant duck: all you do is drown the duck. All they have done is to drag the word DELIGHT down to mean satisfied (or less).

MISSION STATEMENTS ARE PROMISES

Listen, it is no good, as in the case of 'Delighted', writing your aspirations on the vehicles and letter headings. Things like, 'The best in the west', or 'We really care', make you a hostage to those slogans. Although you might see them as jolly little carrots to lure the punters – or if you insist on management speak, 'mission statements' – the customer takes them in an entirely different way, and views them as promises. Promises that, when turned pear-shaped, become a very handy club to beat you with. 'Thank you for calling Garden Chums. We care. I'm Derek, how may I help you?'

'You care?'
'We care.'
'Well then, do you care that one of your guys has just burned my shed down?'

Now you have got to care or the whole thing explodes in your face.

I had personal experience of this the other day when I bought carpets from a large company who had pledged to delight me. There was what I considered to be a fault in the carpet. They told me it was 'reverse pile', a thing about carpets that, although making them about as attractive as a bear's arse, didn't technically constitute a fault. With that in mind, I could jump in the lake as far as they were concerned. They told me I could whinge as much as I liked, but they were under no obligation to offer any solution, and in previous court cases over reverse pile, the customer had been beaten into a penniless pulp. I waited for this little tirade to finish, and said to the thing on the phone:

'But the point is, I am a customer and I am not delighted.'
The reply was belligerent: 'So what?'
'So, your adverts, your vehicles, and your headed notepaper say that I will be delighted, and I am not.'

I won't bore you with the boring and gory details of this conversation, but I finally spoke to the total El Supremo of the whole company:

'I am not delighted.'
'Listen, we can't afford to give in to every customer who comes whinging for their money back.'
'But, then, not all your customers will be delighted.'
'Well quite a few are.'
'Then why doesn't your slogan read: we want a few of you to be delighted?'

The point for you is that to get that edge and to charge those monster prices, you will have to go that extra mile. You will have to dare to ask, 'Mrs Smith, are you really thrilled about the job I have done?'

THE SHEEP AFFAIR

Do you really dare to ask your customers questions in that vein? I come from the heart of the Cotswolds where sheep are important for food, commerce and even romance, and there are one or two clearly defined ways of making money from sheep. One is to cudgel the thing to death, skin it and flog the meat, the hide, and the bones, but you must ask yourself, how often can I skin a sheep? The answer swiftly returns, 'Only once.' Maybe you could look after the sheep, nurse it when it is ill, become its friend and counsel it if it becomes depressed. Then, one hot summer day, it will tell you it is feeling a bit hot in all that wool. 'Would you like me to shear it for you?' 'Baaa, yes please.' How often can you shear a sheep?

Maybe you did a screwy job and you got your hands on the money. Why cause trouble by asking the customer what they thought when you know it was bad? OK, but don't expect to work for that customer again or have them say anything good about you to anyone else. The point is that good husbandry of your stock, be it sheep or customers, makes good sense. Destroying them for profit can only be done once.

THE COST OF LOSING CUSTOMERS

There are two key considerations for us here. Imagine we supply those carpets. In order to secure the job, we have told our customer that they should expect to be delighted. When we hear that they are not delighted, we must at least take a pragmatic view before we give them an aggravating reply, or any reply for that matter. What will it cost us to replace the carpet? What will it cost us not to replace it?

The problem is, that the cost of not replacing it is often hidden. Chilling little facts like, if someone is happy they may tell one other person about it. If they are not happy, they tell 20 others. You will certainly get no repeat business. OK, I have got you convinced. You decide to replace the carpet. Then use it as a positive way to demonstrate your professionalism. Don't say, 'OK, if you're going to yell about it, I suppose I'll have to change it. I don't have to, you know. The big shops would tell you to get lost.' Say with a concerned smile (even if you have murder in your heart), 'I'm sorry you're disappointed. What would you like me to do about it?'

ASK WHAT THEY WOULD LIKE

Did you notice that I said 'What would you like me to do about it?' Sure, the chances are they will want a new carpet or their money back, but they could say 'Well, could you knock a bit off?' and that would make everyone happy. Whatever happens, though, it is important that the customer sees it as part of your friendly, excellent and seamless service.

There is another aspect to this. If you remember, earlier in the book, I talked about how difficult it is to find out the truth about your business. Your friends will lie to save your feelings, I will lie because it is the nature of my profession, but you need to hear the truth and nothing can convey it to you better than a cock-up. If every time you lay a carpet you have to refund the money because of reverse pile, it is going to prove expensive, but if you view this pricey interlude as a learning experience, then it is money well spent. Perhaps reverse pile isn't a recognized fault, but your customers don't like it. So in future you never buy in carpet with reverse pile, even if it means personally examining every one. Whatever you do, from designing power stations to organizing kids' parties, when there is a cock-up you should be able to analyse it and stop it happening again.

MAKING A GREAT IMPRESSION

I know this may seem high-blown for someone starting what they believe to be a modest one-person operation, but it is vital, and I promise that it will pay a premium. Imagine you want your windows cleaned. Someone gives you a phone number on an old betting slip and you ring it:

"'Ello.'
'Oh yes. Do you do window cleaning?'
'Ooose asking?'
'Well I want mine cleaned. I wonder if you could pop round.'
'I can't come out tonight, look, 'cause it's me bingo night.

'When are you in tomorrow?'

'Between 9 and 12.'

'I'll come round about then, look.'

Of course, he doesn't, but shows up two days later, smelling of … well, just smelling. You have seen the rest, so why bore you with the gory details? How could that change?

What about a nice crisp business card with a number that you can ring:

> 'Thank you for calling James Brown Cleaning. How can I help?'
>
> 'Do you clean windows?'
>
> 'We certainly do. Whereabouts are you, and when would you like us to call?'
>
> 'Number 30, High Street. Could you call between 9 and 12?'
>
> 'Certainly. Would 10 past 10 be alright?'
>
> 'Yes.'
>
> 'See you then, and thank you for thinking of us.'

When he arrives, he is uniformed in smart overalls with the James Brown Cleaning logo embroidered on the pockets. He shows you a plastic card with his photograph to confirm who he is (nice move for the older customers). When you ask how much he will charge, he smiles warmly and pulls out a pad with the printed picture on the outside of the four elevations of a house. He draws in the windows and professionally estimates the price. A high price that, with his faultless reliability, you are willing to pay. When a superb job has been done, and you have paid a good price, he gives you a proper receipt and an appointment card for your future calls. Appointments that are kept faultlessly. Before he leaves, he thanks you for your business, checks that you are 'delighted', and invites you to recommend him to your friends.

WAS IT THE BEST COFFEE YOU HAVE EVER TASTED?

I know a lot of you reading this are international business consultants or gourmet restaurateurs, but the same rules apply. If you want to make a lot, your customers will learn to expect a lot, and you can never afford to contradict or sink below these expectations.

Think about this. The last time you went out for the day, you probably stopped at a small café or tea shop for a cup of coffee. There is a good chance that the person running this place was someone like us. Bearing this in mind, ask yourself: was that truly the best coffee you have ever tasted in your life? Was that the most delicious piece of cake you have ever eaten? Of course it won't be. It is the cheapest catering-pack coffee in the nastiest of sanitary-fitting type porcelain cup, with a plastic punnet of chemicals masquerading as milk. It is cold in there, and the staff are stupid kids that are oh so bored. Of course they are doomed, if not to bankruptcy, then certainly to a lifetime of drudgery in a scabby café.

Don't let this little vitriolic tirade intimidate you too much, because even five-star hotels do it. I was invited to present a talk at a conference that was being held in a premier hotel, and at bedtime thought I would indulge myself with the luxury of a hot milky drink. I ordered Ovaltine and it arrived nearly an hour later. It was cold, it was in a cup, (well actually, most of it was in the saucer) and I was bitterly disappointed. OK, it should have been hot and promptly delivered – that is efficient and, if you like, consistent – but even then, remember the pitfalls of BS and ISO. What about bringing it in a proper Ovaltine mug, with its nightcap lid? It would have surprised and delighted me, and that is what you, as a one-person outfit, have the flexibility to do.

Dare to challenge yourself every day about the quality of your performance. Strive always to be a bit better today than you were yesterday. I know that you see me as the jolly cynic who poo-poos all the positive-thinking stuff, but this is the real world where your life depends on getting ahead and staying ahead of the competition. The impression you create sets the price you can charge, or worse, in the case of professional skills, whether you get the work at all. That is why that I now need to touch on the prickly subject of staff training.

VIRTUAL STAFF

'Staff training!' I hear you cry. 'I thought this was a book about jungle warfare, guerrilla tactics, Going-It-Alone, or are you suggesting that I employ a butler to carry my gun?' Well not exactly, but do you remember that earlier on I played with the computer-speak idea of virtual things, and we were able to create a virtual office and a virtual car? Now to create that great money-spinning impression, we need to talk about virtual staff.

Some staff may not be that virtual. If you have a café or shop the chances are that you will need some help, even if it's just some school kids at weekends. But there is the rub. We have agreed that you are to be the best in the world. Well, it kind of contradicts that if your customers are met by a strange, smelly person who looks as though he would like nothing better than to learn the secret of fire. I know this may contradict our hang-loose enjoyment of this project, and fly in the face of the biker-from-hell, business-guru image that I have done so much to cultivate, but yes, I am suggesting that you spend time carefully training these people, particularly on the subject of your aspirations on quality and the desire to be the best. Yes, I am suggesting you set standards for appearance and behaviour to the point of carrying out inspections for shiny shoes and clean fingernails. The fact is that if you start off like this, the scabby people won't want to work for you under those terms.

Train Your Mum

Maybe as a footloose, devil-may-care lone wolf, you won't need to have any staff, but your virtual office will need a virtual receptionist which is quite likely to be your mum, your child or your partner. Imagine the scene. You have visited Sir Nigel. He is nearly convinced that the £50,000 contract is in your grasp. He rings to touch base and iron out a few wrinkles. Your mum answers:

> 'Hello, is that Thunderbolt Catering?'
> 'No, you must have the wrong number. Oh, hang on, you must mean my Alex. He can't speak to you at the moment see, 'cause he's on the toilet.' GAME OVER!

Yes, that's right, you have got to train your mum:

> 'Thank you for calling Thunderbolt Catering, how can I help?'
> 'Yes, I want to speak to Alex Smith.'
> 'Who shall I say is calling?'
> 'Sir Nigel.'
> 'Oh yes, Sir Nigel, he is looking forward to speaking to you, but he is on the other line just at the moment. May I take your number, and he will ring you back in a moment? Yes, I have got that, and thank you for calling. Goodbye.'

Or:

> 'Hello.'
> 'Oh yes, hello, do you do catering?'
> 'I think my dad does, but he ain't here at the moment. Give him a ring back – he might be in after tea.' GAME OVER!

You also need to train your children:

> 'Thank you for ringing Thunderbolt Catering, how may I help?'
> 'I want some catering.'
> 'Certainly, may I ask who's calling? … Yes, Mr Smith … and may I have a phone number? … thank you. Now you say catering, what exactly did you want to discuss? … well that sounds very exciting. I will get Alex Smith to speak to you personally. What is the best time for him to ring you? Thank you for calling.'

You see, we have to delight, thrill, and in every way increase our value by the impression we create.

POINTS TO PONDER

1 If you mug people for their money, smiling afterwards and wishing them 'a nice day' doesn't always put things right. You don't 'do' customer care; you must 'care' about your customers.
2 If you have worked so hard to get these customers, don't forget to work hard to keep them.
3 Don't confuse consistency with quality. The customer decides what quality is by their own standards.
4 If you make a promise to your customers, either face to face, or through some advert or slogan, then understand how furious they will be if you don't keep it.
5 Before you tell a customer to get stuffed, consider carefully how much it will cost you.
6 If you really want the truth, ask an upset customer. It may be news you didn't want to hear, but you needed to hear.
7 Professionalism and kept promises pay premiums.
8 If you create virtual staff, then be prepared to train them, even if it's your mum.

11

Marketing

This is going to be a bit of a toughie because it must be assumed that we are working with a limited budget, and my previous experience of pukka marketing is that it can absorb an unlimited budget. I think, therefore, that we must look at the function of marketing, and see what we can afford to do.

If any of you out there are marketing gurus, you may wince at my definitions, but this is supposed to be a practical survival guide, so pure it ain't. Marketing is about finding markets. It can tell us what market we should be in, where to find it, where it can find us, and how to get the best out of it when this happens. The publicity side of it will tell the world, or the bit of the world we are interested in at any rate, that we exist and that we have a great deal to offer, in both senses of the word 'deal'.

SEE THE FUTURE THROUGH THE MAGIC RUNES OF MARKETING

At the very start of our enterprise, marketing can even help us decide what business we should be getting involved in. Let's just review for a moment some of the pitfalls we discussed earlier. The cock-up caused by reading the marketing information incorrectly was exemplified by the guy who calculated through statistics that there were no shops selling handmade chocolate in a community of redundant miners, and saw it as a business opportunity. This was perhaps an aberration (it certainly was for the guy who sank his savings into it), but more commonly, we encountered people who had overstretched themselves right at the start, with too much borrowing and leasing to fund their dream.

When I had a proper day job in marketing, the high-flying mega-companies used two types of marketing that could be very helpful to us mere mortals. These were 'slipstream' and, more usefully, 'asset' marketing. Slipstream is exactly what it means. For a long time, my family has possessed one of those bizarre French contraptions, laughingly known as a Citroen 2CV car. Despite being a four-door saloon, these things only have a 600 cc engine, and the suicidal but efficient way to make swift progress on the motorway is to lock in tight behind a speeding juggernaut lorry, which pulls you along. In France a few years ago, when everybody drove the things, every lorry would have a parasitic wobbly car a few centimetres from its fender.

The same can be done by the small business. We saw it with the burger bar that looked like a chain franchise and wasn't. He would not have succeeded if he had been the first burger outlet that anyone had seen. In fact, an American had come to our town a few years earlier, and opened the Genuine Texas Burger Bar. It fell flat because he was a one-man operation trying to do a product launch well outside his financial reach.

If you take weird things like sundried tomatoes, freshly squeezed orange juice, Indian spices or mangetout peas, the big supermarkets are doing loss-making pioneering for us, and we can slipstream in to sell our exotics without the cost of an education programme. If it is the international business consultant route for you, it takes a little more subtlety, but the principle is the same.

I will change the names and details to avoid being sued, but there is a major business consultancy that has got itself into a bit of an argy-bargy over tax. At first I thought that the tax authorities were being petty in pursuing the individual consultants for tax on their day-to-day petty cash until I read that individuals could claim as much as a million a year. Now even if you are reading this book in the year 2025, I bet a million a year would be alright as an income, let alone as out-of-pocket petty-cash expenses. The point

I am trying to make here is that as regards business consultancy, our large competitors have already educated the potential client to expect mega-bills. When I work with these people I am often embarrassed and uneasy about how really very junior consultants (and us) are always provided with first-class or at least business-class air travel, cars with drivers and top-class hotels. I can hardly say to my clients, give me the cash and I'll hitchhike or kip in the car, but if I did, that would be a reasonable income in itself.

IF YOUR COMPETITORS CHARGE BIG BUCKS, SO CAN YOU

So, why can't *you* charge those sorts of prices? The answer is you can, but things get a bit more complicated here because you will have some tricky decisions. I am a bit nervous about taking the responsibility for you making what could be very expensive and disastrous decisions, so don't blame me for this (if you do, I shall say you should have taken up window cleaning). The technique that we combine with slipstream marketing is 'benchmarking'. In other words, if you want to charge what the others do, you must look, behave and do what the others do. It's no good appearing in your M&S or Sears, when they are in Savile Row or Gucci. You can't present in a plastic ring-binder if they are in red leather.

Now you can start to see the problem, but to be fair, also the opportunity because a senior consultant can buy a Savile Row suit for the cost of one day's consultancy. The problem is that it is chicken and egg: do you mortgage your home to buy a suit in the hope of getting work? Maybe this should suggest that you should present as well as possible, and save the major jobs until you can work up to them.

THE OTHER PATHWAY

On the other hand, there is another path, sadly even more dangerous, but it is the one I have chosen, and one I revel in. Maybe on a car journey you have felt somewhat put out by those dark, snarling motorcycles that make the rider adopt the stance of a chimp (the bikes are called Street Fighters, by the way). Well, don't be too condemnatory because one of them could well be me on my beloved 1,000-cc bike called Gladys, blasting off to visit clients. It may seem chancy at first, but we discussed this car thing before. Imagine, then, as the client judges us by walking along the cars in his car park: 'L, LX, GLi, L, GS, 1,000-cc Street Fighter?' They can't place it.

The danger is that you need position before you can pull a stunt like that. You literally risk everything. There are a lot who have pulled it off, and a lot who haven't. I managed to get into the daily papers as the Hell's Angel business consultant. Nigel Kennedy became famous as the punk violinist, Jean-Paul Gaultier, French fashion designer, wears a kilt and Doc Martens, and John McEnroe hurled abuse.

These are very high-risk strategies, but they do get you noticed. You don't get headlines like, 'Man in smart blue suit to advise bank,' or 'Tennis player in clean white shorts shakes hands with umpire,' it's 'Man bites dog' all over again. But, play these games at your peril, and don't blame me if the world thinks you're a prat. Perhaps it is better to be safe than sorry, so ...

SLIPSTREAM AND BENCHMARK

Let them do the work. Pinch their best ideas, and improve on them. Don't pioneer unless you don't mind losing your shirt.

ASSET MARKETING

Strangely enough, we have something in common with huge corporations, and that is that we are strapped for cash. In our cases it's tens we are short of, and in theirs it is tens of millions, but the problem and the solution are the same.

A really jumbo cost for the big companies is developing and launching new products. Because of this, a discipline called asset marketing has been developed. The idea is that you audit the company's assets in terms of product, capacity, distribution and expertise, and you only develop a product that uses these assets, hopefully taking up slack in under-utilized ones.

The textbook example is Kellogg's, who desperately wanted some new breakfast cereals but didn't want to invest wads of wonga. The marketing gurus audited the assets and discovered certain facts:

1 There was always capacity in the Cornflake production bit.
2 There was a need in the novelty cereal market.

From this, they decided to sugar-coat the existing Cornflakes, sprinkle them with nuts and, bingo, the yummy and successful Crunchy Nut Cornflakes were born with little initial investment.

A more dramatic example was the Quaker Oat Corporation, whose audit revealed that they had an excellent distribution network, the ability to make colourful packaging, and a talent to market to kids through the adult decision maker. The new product had to be sensitive to the Quaker non-violence ethic, and from all of this, 'Fisher Price Toys' was born. Think about it. Clever hey?

AND THE KITCHEN SINK

Now what about you? What assets have you got? A car, a kitchen, a garage, typewriter, home computer, a phone? Then don't offer crop spraying because few of your assets will be utilized. Make scrummy sandwiches and deliver them in the car, and your existing assets are used. But don't forget that your current skills are also assets, so it may be a mistake to abandon them entirely. If you are a dress designer, an accountancy practice may be a mistake.

Having said that, this book is being mainly written to help set you free, and to let you enjoy your life. If you don't enjoy being a brain surgeon, and you want to train elephants then GO FOR IT! Just remember that there will be a cost, although it may be one worth paying.

TELLING THE WORLD

Now that marketing has chosen our path, we must use it to tell the world about us. We can choose advertising, telesales campaigns, direct mail and PR, and if we use professionals to do it for us it can cost a fortune. If we do it ourselves, it can be crap, so the KEY here is professional presentation with amateur costs.

As we saw earlier, professional design may be essential. Again, I don't want to take responsibility for the consequences of saying this so I won't, but if instead of buying a £15,000 car you feel is an essential part of your business you spend 15 grand on advertising, the benefits might surprise you. For heaven's sake, don't rush out and do it. Just think about the priorities of where you spend your money. Personally, I would spend a grand on my publicity, nothing on the car, and then know that for 14 grand I could survive for nearly a year while things got going.

I have already said that beautiful business cards and headed notepaper give the impression of the assets that we don't necessarily have, and of course, the same will apply to the production of our advertising and publicity material. This really is an area where you must use cleverness and guile to compensate for a lack of money. Perhaps you will rake all your meagre savings together to launch yourself with some local advertising, and you find that the newspaper charges £250 for a quarter page. Desperate to make a splash, you bite the bullet and sign up for it. What about another £500 to design it? This you don't do because the newspaper's sales representative can put something 'snappy' together for you.

ATTENTION

As I have already mentioned, there is a new, toe-curling horribleness that has seeped up between the cracks in society. It is called 'clip art', and it means that every type-generating computer has a library of naff, passé, kitsch, horrid little pictures. So when you see your ad, there will be a cartoon prat with a megaphone with a big wobbly 'ATTENTION' coming out of it.

Advertising tells the punter something, and you have just told them you are a tatty cheapskate. Be very careful. Look at the best ad and pinch their idea. A very naughty thing you can do, which is a sort of fraud that is not illegal even if it is immoral, is to go to a great advertising agency and invite them to pitch for your publicity launch. They have to submit good ideas to win the business. I don't think much of doing that, despite its effectiveness. A solution which is just as effective, but lets you sleep at night, is to go to an art college and offer a prize like a new mountain bike or colour television to the student who can design the most exciting publicity for a small company setting up. The commercial colleges often welcome projects like this, the students like the prizes, and you get 40-odd fabulous modern designs for very little money.

You should spend time working out precisely what impression you need to make. For now then, as regards adverts:

- Be well designed.
- Be precise.
- Know exactly what impression you want to create, and check that an independent person agrees that you have succeeded.

This doesn't mean you can't do it on the cheap, it just means you need to know what you want. The press ad will go out to 99.9 per cent of people who have no interest in you or what you offer. If you know whom you are aiming at, you can save a fortune.

READY, FIRE, AIM

When I first finished college, I had an urgent need of funds, and my asset audit told me I had nothing other than an old van. This meant I had a delivery business to market. Two cheap marketing strategies soon had funds rolling in. Firstly, I bought a white coat and had in two-inch-high letters the word 'TRANSPORT' embroidered on the back by my mum. With this on, I just stood around at furniture auctions and, without fail, 20 or 30 people would approach me to arrange the transport of their purchases. Secondly, I placed an advert in the 'items for sale' section of the local evening newspaper every night. It simply stated: 'All items in this column can be delivered,' and the phone rang off the hook every night. I think the reason it worked was that it was specifically aimed at my target audience.

Much later, when it came to promoting my training and consultancy business, certain things worked far better than others. As Sherlock Holmes said to poor old Watson one day, 'You see, but you do not observe,' and as regards self-promotion, may I dare to suggest that you, dear reader, are currently seeing but not observing? Would you like to hire me personally to come and help you get your business started? What did you say? You would like to but you don't think you could afford to? Why? Do you think that I am likely to be expensive because I am a famous business author, read worldwide by royalty and the captains of industry? I wonder what gave you that impression. Maybe it is because you are at this moment reading my book: the best bit of publicity I could wish for. Otherwise, I am no different to you. Tom Peters is no different to you, or Richard Branson, Bill Gates or Delia Smith. They have just used the publicity of their own publicity, as it were, to gather pace like a snowball.

Obviously you need to start somewhere, but then again, so did all the people on that list.

IF YOU'VE GOT IT, FLAUNT IT

The method for me that paid the highest dividend was straight, unabashed self-publicity. I developed a very light-hearted 10-minute presentation on my subject, and offered my body to all the local business clubs, business breakfast meetings, chambers of commerce and commercial exhibitions. OK, so you give away some precious time, but at the start, time is something that there is a bit of! It doesn't matter what you do – icing cakes, tax advice, aircraft design or making wedding dresses – there is a group some-where dying to see you. The only problem that I found was catch-ing 250 people to pin them down afterwards. To this end I would leave a reply-paid card on every seat and I would always get 20 or 30 or so back, which would nearly all turn into business.

The reply-paid cards were originally designed to send out, which to start with I did in batches of 1,000, to targeted compa-nies. This would result in 15 solid jobs. That is only a 1.5 per cent response, which I am told is quite good for mailers. The cost made it just about worthwhile, but not nearly as effective as the per-sonal appearances. As things turned out, the personal appearances have become the day job. Oh well, you can never tell can you?

THEIR PICTURE IS NEVER OUT OF THE PAPERS

Finally, in the same vein, make sure you take every opportunity to get in the press, and on local radio. Don't think this is diffi-cult. They are desperate for business news, and anyway, they really can't be bothered to say no if you pester them. Even national newspapers, radio and television are not as hard to pen-etrate as you think. You just need two things: the nerve to approach them and something a little bit different to hang your hat on. I have got the 'Hell's Angel business guru' thing. You could be the nude house painter, the accountant who sky dives into every job, the dress designer who eats live bats, or whatever. The only thing that is surprising is that the phone does not ring off the hook the very next morning.

When I managed to get my happy, smiling face in a prestige Sunday paper for the first time, I sat back and waited for the hordes of marauding fans to gather, but there were just about half a dozen calls. Out of three million readers, that is a bit dreary, but then I found that the world and its dog had seen it. Appointments were easier to get, conversations were a breeze and I had so much less of a task proving my credibility. Good PR unlocks the door, but you still have to push at it.

POINTS TO PONDER

1 Let your competitor educate the customers to expect what you are offering.
2 If you dare take the risk, there can be money in getting noticed (just don't blame me if there's trouble).
3 Audit the assets you have (skills, knowledge or physical possessions) and try to utilize them before investing in things you don't possess.
4 Non-professional design and presentation make you look like an amateur. Definition: 'someone who does it for nothing'.
5 Advertising is used to say something about you. Be careful it doesn't say you are sad, skint and desperate.
6 If you haven't got cash coming out of your ears, use your 'intelligence' to be precise in your targeting of customers.
7 Get yourself noticed by being around the right places and talking yourself up.
8 Never be out of the news, be it local papers, trade magazines, radio or television. It's not at all difficult. Just make yourself a bit of a nuisance.

The Zen of Going-It-Alone

One of my favourite books is that already-mentioned hippy classic, *Zen and the Art of Motorcycle Maintenance* by Robert Pirsig. Although, as I said, it gets a bit heavy going and a lot of people don't finish it, it does contain some great ideas. The one for us now is the idea of 'stuckness', as Pirsig calls it. While dealing with a catastrophic breakdown with his motorcycle (and with his personality, as it happens) he shows it to be a great-mind expanding opportunity.

To translate it for us, living up until now has been about trundling on, day in, day out, towards retirement and death. Oh, happy day! That was the life. And you say you miss it? Maybe you indulged in a bit of DIY, some amateur dramatics, ethnic weaving or steamy bondage sessions, but you know the name for these. They are called pastimes, they pass time, the one valuable, irreplaceable asset you have. You waste it by passing days at a turgid job. Then the evening and weekends you spend passing the time until you can get back to it. Some of you may have lost that job. Perhaps you mourn that loss and wonder what now. Mourn it like the loss of a boil and come with me to get stuck into a bit of stuckness.

Imagine that each day you leave a room by way of the door. You just turn the door handle, open the door, and you are out, but then the fateful day arrives and the handle comes off in your hand. This is stuckness, you are stuck, but you also have a great opportunity, a great new vista opens up of things you hadn't previously considered or even understood. How do door handles work? Sure the handle's motion is circular but whatever is inside the door moves from side to side. Is there any other way of moving it? The point is that you are now gaining knowledge of door mechanisms. Perhaps you could leave the room by another route. What about the window? This gives us a keener insight into our environment with lateral opportunities we hadn't previously explored. Is there someone on the other side of the door who could help? Can we communicate with them to help us? This way we are learning communication skills and we are networking. And, finally, did we really want to leave the room anyway?

THE OTHER SIDE OF THE WALL

Perhaps when you had a proper day job, the work you had to do came through a hole in the wall, and when you had inscribed the do-hicky and retabulated the scriver scale, you would pass the job through another hole in the wall. It is like our door knob, an apparently inconsequential device that we used without thinking, but now we have to see how it works. You now will have the fun of finding out what was on the other side of those walls.

When you leave the job, or the job leaves you, it may seem a tiny bit more catastrophic than the loss of the door handle, but the effect is the same. You will experience the glorious opportunity of stuckness. Over the last few thousand words that we have shared together, I have attempted, if you like, to be the person on the other side of that handle-less door. Your success will come partially from your core skills, be it hairdressing, hamster breeding or time-machine design, but in your previous life, lots of different people would handle those other-side-of-the-wall jobs for you. Mr Biggins of sales would send his team of reps countrywide to drum up demand for time machines. Mrs Higiss from procurement would ensure you had a chair to sit on. Although this may have seemed a happy situation because it set you free to get on with the job in hand, the problem was that all these people drew a wage, had to have chairs to sit on, light, heat, and even free cars, all drawn from the sweat of your brow.

A JACK OR JILL OF ALL TRADES

Now you are Going-It-Alone, you must expand your horizons to master the ancillary skills. If you are truly worried about your ability to cope with them, don't think going without these skills is an option. If you make novelty clothes pegs and they aren't actively sold, you will end up buried under 50 tons of novelty clothes pegs. What you can do, however, is hire in those skills that you really can't cope with. You may notice that we haven't exactly spent a lot of time on tax, book-keeping and financial management. This is because, for me, book-keeping is about as easy as nailing a jelly to the ceiling. This doesn't mean that it isn't important, and I have spent a great deal of my hard-earned cash on having it scrupulously done for me, but that has to be added to my overhead, and my selling of myself has to be even more proficient. A lot of the 'start your own business' books deal solely with the financial management aspect, and if you can master them as well, your horizons will be even broader than mine.

On the subject of the other business books, be a little careful. Some are even published by banks! They all start off with the basic assumption that you know what 'enterprise' (as they call it) you want to set up, or even that you want to start it at all. If, after reading my book, you decide that all this Go-It-Alone stuff isn't for you, I have done a good job. This, in my mind, was to be a gritty survival guide for the individual out there on his or her own. I wanted, as I wrote each section, to find the key elements that would truly and utterly secure success, or at least guarantee an avoidance of failure and disaster. Well, one way to avoid financial ruin in an ill-founded 'enterprise' is not to do it in the first place, and if that is what I have persuaded you to do, that's well and good.

HELP YOURSELF

There has been one genuine source of contention between my editor and me, and that is on the subject of self-help books and positive thinking. In fact, you will remember at the start of this book, I had quite a wild tirade against them, and ever since, my editor has been asking for a retraction because she genuinely believes them to be useful. To go some of the way to meet her, I have also found them useful, books like *How to Win Friends and Influence People* by Dale Carnegie, *Think and Grow Rich* by Napoleon Hill and, a bit more cerebrally, *The Successful Self* by Dorothy Rowe.

My problem is that when you don't succeed, these books can turn around and bite you. If you buy 'I Cured My Athlete's Foot by Learning to Love Myself', each day you would do your 'I love myself' mantra and thank each toe for supporting you throughout your life. All this is conducted with a beatific smile until, one day, the athlete's foot disappears. From that day forward, when friends tell you in confidence of this unfortunate fungal infection of their toes, you can smile a pious smile and nod understandingly while knowing in your heart that they don't believe in themselves. Then the fateful day comes. Did you notice just a touch of tingly itching in one of your toes? 'No, no, no!' you secretly scream, 'I believe, I believe.' The others in your toe-support group give you that same sickening but knowing smile when you 'confess'.

This book is not such a book. Of course you would do well to have self-belief and self-confidence, but it isn't essential. If you take the practical, cautious steps set down, you should succeed, and if you do screw up, you haven't let the book down. You certainly haven't let yourself down. You haven't broken a magic spell. You just screwed up. Let's pick up the bits, put it back together, and avoid ever making that mistake again. End of story.

Some self-employed people are seen from the outside as working too hard, and they are accused of doing nothing but work, or living for their jobs. Consider the person in that paid job who has to indulge in those pastimes and then think about the miller whom we met at the start of this book. The trick is he hasn't got a job, he has a lifestyle. He is the miller, he is the blacksmith or the farmer. They don't stop work, sure, but then they don't really start. They never retire, but they can start to take things easy.

If you really are going to do this thing, I bet you are nervous and a little unsure, but if you crack it, your whole life will blossom and bear fruit in a way that no day job could let you. Just remember to make a great impression on people, dare to hear the real truth about yourself and your ideas (remember poor old Rent a Rodent?). When you are the best in the world, don't be afraid to charge the best prices in the world. Remember there is only one of you, one unique you – that scarcity should make you dearer, not cheaper. Just make sure you are the best. Don't worry, though. If you are prepared to listen, disgruntled customers will soon tell you when you are not. Don't be afraid to ask people to buy things, and don't be afraid to tell the whole world you exist.

I really hope all this has been some use to you, and that you have enjoyed the time we have spent together. It would thrill me if what you have just shared with me really brought you what you feel is success, and piece of mind. Remember, because it is important to me to succeed at what I do (which is writing this), I am really wishing you success.

GOOD LUCK
AND ALL THE BEST
FROM
GEOFF BURCH

Further Reading

Eric Berne, *Games People Play* (Penguin, 1970).

Geoff Burch, *Resistance is Useless* (Headline, 1994).

Dale Carnegie, *How to Win Friends and Influence People* (Mandarin, 1990).

John Fenton, *Close, Close, Close* (Mercury, 1990).

Charles Handy, All his books.

Harry Harrison, *Stainless Steel Rat* (Millenium, 1997).

Napoleon Hill, *Think and Grow Rich* (Thorsons, 1996).

Tom Peters, All his books have got something to offer (published by Macmillan).

Michael Pirsig, *Zen and the Art of Motorcycle Maintenance* (Vintage, 1991).

Dorothy Rowe, *The Successful Self* (Fontana, 1989).

Index

and use of own name 85–6
franchising 86–7
freedom 1–2, 10, 35, 188
future, planning 37

hedgehog close, in sales 140–1
hiring 74–5
honesty 73–4
hourly rates 41–2

idea *see* new ideas
image, investing in 79–81
improvement 153
individualism 185–6, 191–2
information-gathering 123, 138–41,
    151–3
innovation 18–19
investigation phase, use of
    questions 145–53

job description, writing down, to
    avoid failure 37
job satisfaction 4–5
job security xi-xii, 46
justification, avoiding 142–3

labels 35
learning-curve, charging for 14–15,
    16
leases 45–6, 54–5, 63
letters 124
life-energy *see* time
lifestyle:
    auditing 22, 24
    costing xii-xiv
    work as 23–5, 196–7
linked sales 162–3
listening 125–6, 138–43, 150
loneliness 66

market intelligence 29–30, 153,
    183–4

marketing 183–92
mission statements 107, 174–5
money up front 43–5, 72
mortgages 45–6, 76

name, for undertaking 83–6
negotiating, and sales 105
new ideas 18–19
    truthful reviews 27–30, 197
noticed, getting 185–6, 191–2
nouveaux riches 71

objections:
    handling, with questions 156
    as sign of interest 157–9
    unspoken 154–6
objectives 113–14
    achieving 123–37
    staging 127–9, 132–4
office, virtual 67
open questions 139–43
optimism 54, 62, 87
overgearing 48, 163, 184

partners, and self-employment
    24–5, 32–3
partnerships 8
past, and introductory questions
    148
patents 18
personal appearances 191
personal recommendation 19, 178
persuasiveness 126
    questions in 147, 152
photocopying 75
place, ideal, for making sales 136–7
plan of action, in sales technique
    149, 161
power:
    from questions 149, 150–2
    and self-employment 31–2
premises 45–6